How to
PROFIT
in
GOLD

How to
PROFIT
in
GOLD

Professional Tips and Strategies for Today's Ultimate Safe Haven Investment

JONATHAN SPALL

New York Chicago San Francisco Lisbon London Madrid Mexico City
Milan New Delhi San Juan Seoul Singapore Sydney Toronto

The *McGraw·Hill* Companies

Portions of this work have appeared previously in the book *Investing in Gold: The Essential Safe Haven Investment for Every Portfolio* by Jonathan Spall (McGraw-Hill, 2009).

1 2 3 4 5 6 7 8 9 10   DOC/DOC   1 9 8 7 6 5 4 3 2 1 0

ISBN   978-0-07-175195-7
MHID   0-07-175195-5

This publication is designed to provide accurate and authoritative information in regard to the subject matter covered. It is sold with the understanding that neither the author nor the publisher is engaged in rendering legal, accounting, securities trading, or other professional services. If legal advice or other expert assistance is required, the services of a competent professional person should be sought.
  —*From a Declaration of Principles Jointly Adopted by a Committee of the American Bar Association and a Committee of Publishers and Associations*

McGraw-Hill books are available at special quantity discounts to use as premiums and sales promotions or for use in corporate training programs. To contact a representative, please e-mail us at bulksales@mcgraw-hill.com.

This book is printed on acid-free paper.

In Memoriam
Jack Spall
1930–2009

Contents

Preface   ix

Acknowledgments   xi

1   Gold at Record Highs   1

2   What Drives the Price of Gold?   9

3   The Official Sector   25

4   Lenders and Borrowers of Gold   53

5   Bullion Banks   65

6   Gold Exchanges   93

7   Exchange-Traded Funds   109

8   Physical Gold   115

9   Gold: Myths and Reality   123

10   Getting Exposure to Gold   137

Appendix A: "Rules" for Trading Gold   147

Appendix B: Frequently Asked
             Questions   149

Appendix C: Glossary of Terms   163

Appendix D: Properties of Gold   193

Appendix E: Bar Weights and
             Their Agreed
             Fine Gold Content   199

             Index   201

Preface

I believe that too many books on the gold market concentrate on theory and some notion of how it ought to operate. I am not an academic, and I have no research background—in fact, I recently sat eating dim sum with a friend from the market, and we were giggling at the notion that there are people who believe that supply and demand are always the prime determinants of moves in the gold price just as if it was a normal "commodity." All highly childish, and while they are the drivers from time to time, they are most certainly not always, and when they are, it is generally a very short-lived phenomenon. My knowledge of this field is firsthand, and to write this book on what interests traders, how the market works, and what dealers concentrate on, I have drawn upon the experience I gained working in a trading room for a living.

I started my full-time career in the gold market in 1983. Apart from the odd foray as a foreign exchange and bond trader, this is what I have spent my working life doing—trading and talking to customers about precious metals markets. Over the last 27 years or so, I have been employed by four of the world's largest banks and always for those that have had a strong position in this market.

During my career I have lived and worked in New York, London, Hong Kong, and Sydney. I have been an interbank market maker on three continents, and I have traveled to 70 or so nations to meet with central banks and finance ministries to discuss the outlook for gold. I have sat with mining companies to debate hedging strategies and traveled over a mile underground to see the ore being extracted. Currently the majority of my time is spent talking to those involved with hedge, pension, and sovereign wealth funds on the events surrounding the recent extraordinary rise in the metal's price.

While I believe there is a strong argument that gold has been money for thousands of years and that the events of the last 20 years or so, including our obsession with paper money and ever-increasing levels of complexity, could well have been an aberration, I have resisted the temptation to delve into Egyptians, Aztecs, and Incas. Many authors are far more interested in this than I, and they will have covered this field so much better.

Therefore, this book contains very little about the history of gold. Instead, it is much more about how professional traders operate and the types of factors that influence their decision making. It also covers the various exchanges that they use and generally how the gold market works.

In this updated version of my book I have dispensed with the chapters on mining and refining and instead have concentrated much more on the events behind the rally in gold and what could once more propel the market to fresh all-time highs.

Acknowledgments

How to Profit in Gold builds and expands on a number of themes that were originally explored in *Investing in Gold*, which was published by McGraw-Hill in December 2008. This book keeps many of these threads and in particular how bank traders view the gold market and how they operate— so many of the acknowledgments remain exactly the same. However, I would like to single out Suki Cooper of the Commodities Research team at Barclays Capital for particular thanks in putting together the various charts that underscore my arguments as well as Philip Klapwijk of GFMS, Matt Graydon of the World Gold Council, and Matthew Turner of Virtual Metals for allowing me to reproduce their updated data.

As before, I would like to thank my father for instilling a love of this most compelling, and often quirky, investment, although sadly he did not live to see this book published, and I'd like to thank my family for putting up with my absences and fits of pique when things did not exactly go according to plan!

To my many colleagues, friends, customers, and competitors in the market, I would like to offer my wholehearted appreciation for the banter and the sparring as we tried to beat each other up during the trading day and yet managed friendship and socializing after work. You are too numerous to mention individually so I am not even going to bother to try. However, these people are based all over the world, in every continent bar Antarctica, and they extend from my near 19 years of working in the London market, through to 6 years in Hong Kong, and 3 years in Sydney.

It would be nice to think that in my time in this industry I had developed total recall and a perfect knowledge, but this is sadly untrue. I have had to search back through my notes and recollections before ultimately approaching a number of people in the business for assistance with data and information.

I am grateful for the assistance of Jessica Cross and her team at Virtual Metals as well as Stewart Murray of the LBMA.

I also thank the International Monetary Fund (Patricia Loo), the European Central Bank (Regina Schuller), Dennis Gartman, TOCOM (Tony Crane), NYMEX (Jenifer Semenza), The Chinese Gold and Silver Exchange Society (Cynthia Chan), the Shanghai Futures Exchange (Cui Tong), the Dubai Commodity Exchange (Colin Griffith), and The London Gold Market Fixing Ltd.

In addition, I would like to thank GATA (Chris Powell), No Dirty Gold (Payal Sampat), and ARM (Catalina Cock).

Finally, I would like to thank Jennifer Ashkenazy, Jane Palmieri, and their colleagues at McGraw-Hill for their support and encouragement during this second undertaking.

1

Gold at Record Highs

In 1999 gold was friendless. Having reached its then all-time high of $850 some 19 years earlier, it instead languished at $250 and looked almost certain to break lower. Indeed, in a world where clicks were more important than bricks, gold symbolized everything that many of the dot-coms turned out not to be. It had a long track record, it physically existed, and if dropped on your foot, it most definitely hurt. However, this counted for nothing where all the talk was of derivatization and highly structured products.

Even central banks, whose mandate is normally preservation of wealth, had decided to abandon this traditional element of their reserves in favor of assets that yielded a return. In 1997 Australia sold gold, and two years later both Switzerland and the United Kingdom announced that they too were going to be drastically reducing the percentage of precious metals held in their reserves.

The market's shock and dismay was not just that three nations had decided to curtail their investments in gold but that it was those three countries that had been assumed to be favorably disposed to gold. Previously the market had endured selling from Belgium, the Netherlands, Malaysia, Brazil, and others, but these were the then third largest gold producer (Australia), the country where the benchmark for gold is set twice each day (the United Kingdom), and the home of conservative banking and discreet private wealth (Switzerland). The logic ran that if these central banks were selling their gold reserves, then clearly the entire holdings of the official sector were at imminent risk of being liquidated.

It was against this background of extreme pessimism that 15 central banks announced the first European central bank Gold Agreement (EcbGA) in September 1999—covered in depth in Chapter 3. This agreement crystallized their intentions for gold and timetabled sales to minimize market disruption. Ultimately the U.K. government sold 395 tonnes* of gold at an average of around $275. As an aside, it is worth noting that the United Kingdom differs from other countries in that the U.K. government owns the nation's reserves rather than the central bank, which is more normally the case. The media's opprobrium for these sales at near 30-year lows is generally laid firmly at the feet of the then chancellor of the exchequer (finance minister), and later prime minister, Gordon Brown.

It was the announcement on November 2, 2009, that the Reserve Bank of India had bought 200 tonnes of gold at an average price of around $1,045 that neatly demonstrated just how much the fortunes of gold had changed over a 10-year period. Indeed, the news of India's paying nearly four times as much per ounce as the United Kingdom had achieved in its sales, plus the much smaller purchases from the International Monetary Fund (IMF) by Sri Lanka (10 tonnes) and Mauritius (2 tonnes), showed that the nature of the debate had changed and it was no longer about which country might be selling its gold but instead which might be buying. China and

---

*Throughout this book I have used the spelling tonnes rather than tons to refer to metric tons because tonne is the term used globally in the gold market and because the spelling ton is ambiguous: it could refer variously to the metric ton, the American short ton, or the British long ton, which are three rather different quantities. The term tonne is unambiguous in that it always refers to the metric ton.

Russia were the names generally bandied about, but Brazil was seen as another potential candidate to purchase the remaining 191.3 tonnes being offered by the IMF. This debate is covered later.

So what had changed in the intervening period?

In 1980, gold rose to its then heady heights of $850 per troy ounce on a combination of inflationary concerns, the oil price, and the Russians' having marched into Afghanistan (Figure 1-1). Silver price increases were even more rampant, managing to reach some $49 per ounce in nominal terms, a level that it has never seriously challenged since. In that environment of fear, energy rationing, and uncertainty, gold was the natural destination for investors.

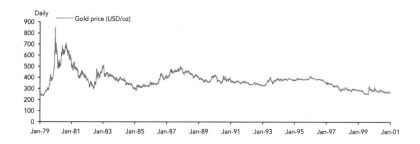

Figure 1-1

Performance of Gold from 1979 to 2001

Source: EcoWin and Barclays Capital

However, by the late 1990s, it was clear that gold no longer resonated as a financial investment for the vast majority of people. The Cold War was over, and energy prices were low. In a world dominated by news of technological discoveries, why would anyone have been interested in such a low-tech opportunity? In addition to central bank selling, the market was dominated by the hedging—accelerated selling—of the gold producers and the war of words that raged between the miners and the central banks over who should take the blame for the demise of gold.

Moreover, the stock of central bankers was at its zenith. The actions of Paul Volcker as chairman for the Federal Reserve (from 1979 to 1987) and Karl Otto Poehl as president of Germany's Bundesbank (1980 to 1991) probably exemplified the no-nonsense policies that were, at the time, credited with bringing inflation under control. This was a period when economies could seemingly be directed fairly easily and growth was assured. In turn, this group of central bankers gave way to no lesser reputations than Alan Greenspan in the United States and Schlesinger, Tietmeyer, and Welteke in Germany. Looking at a chart of gold for this period, it is easy to see just how much gold underperformed inflation. So although there were price pressures at this time, it was assumed that a few words, and perhaps an adjustment to interest rates, were all that was needed for matters to resume their course.

The chart in Figure 1-2 illustrates the poor performance of gold at this time, due to what might be characterized as a trust bonanza: a peak in the widely held belief in the efficacy and omnipotence of monetary policy.

Indeed, gold was so marginalized that it seemed little could be done to rescue it. Admittedly the European central banks had done

Figure 1-2

Gold's Performance Relative to U.S. Inflation

Source: EcoWin and Barclays Capital

their best to remove uncertainty by timetabling their selling (covered in depth in Chapter 3). Moreover, various mining companies announced their intention not to hedge—thus removing many concerns about an overhang of selling above the market. However, by the time the planes flew into the World Trade Center on 9/11/2001, gold was still languishing. There was some hedge fund buying of gold that day but very little—few people had the appetite for much more than stunned horror anyway—and ultimately gold could not hold its gains.

During George W. Bush's reelection campaign in 2004, Al-Qaeda released a tape calling for fresh attacks on the United States. Political commentators were divided as to whether this was an election advantage for Bush or John Kerry. Currency markets were similarly split in their interpretation as to who would benefit. In this confusion the dollar did not move. Obviously, though, the market was clearly bullish for gold: uncertainty, elections, attacks. However, the market's lack of confidence was so great that it could not even react to such a significant piece of news, as it was simply wedded to the fate of the U.S. dollar. When that failed to react, gold could not overcome the obstacle.

The chart in Figure 1-3 shows the gold price in euro terms for this period. I have chosen this chart because it strips out the impact of moves in the U.S. dollar—gold tends to run counter to the dollar,

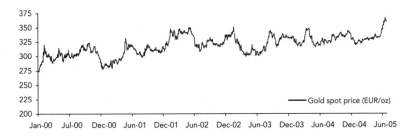

Figure 1-3

Price of Gold Denominated in Euros from 2000 to Mid-2005

Source: EcoWin and Barclays Capital

and showing price movements in euros is a much better indicator of trends that have taken place in the metal itself rather than external factors.

Apart from the occasional blip, and more significantly toward the end of the period, it is clear that gold generally failed to resonate with investors, with the metal's moving up just 18 percent in five and a half years.

The chart in Figure 1-4 is the same chart as in Figure 1-3 except that it shows the trends for mid-2005 to 2010, and that is a very different picture with the gold price multiplying by some 2.5 times.

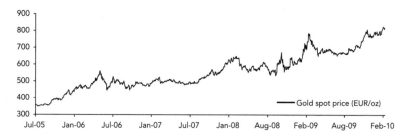

Figure 1-4

Price of Gold Denominated in Euros from Mid-2005 to Early 2010

Source: EcoWin and Barclays Capital

So what changed? From being a forgotten asset, why did gold rally nearly threefold in U.S. dollars as well? See Figure 1-5.

In many ways it became a circular argument—the consistent weakness of the U.S. currency saw gold benefit being coupled with huge pools of investment money looking for new opportunities and commodities being increasingly viewed as an acceptable asset class. Finally, there was growing distrust in the infallibility of monetary authorities, along with a desire for investments that are clear-cut and simple to understand and that are not dependent on a fortunate set of outcomes or an abstruse branch of mathematics.

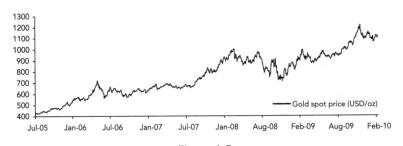

Figure 1-5

Price of Gold in U.S. Dollars from Mid-2005 to Early 2010

Source: EcoWin and Barclays Capital

These features plus the monetary authorities' being forced to cut interest rates in the face of one financial crisis after another, even while the media trumpeted the return of inflation, all helped to create the perfect storm for gold—indeed, many central banks seemed to have little policy other than a desperate desire to avoid deflation. If that sounds extreme, then a conversation with almost any of those institutions over the last few years would disabuse you—many believe that they have the tools to deal with even aggressive inflation, but they admit that they are clueless when confronted with deflation. The "trust bonanza" had become the "trust gap."

To be sure, if asked for a shopping list of conditions to ensure a rally in gold, recent events have pretty much checked off every one. These conditions resulted in gold's making record nominal highs of EUR 812.50 and USD 1,226 on December 3, 2009. However, on February 19, 2010, gold traded above EUR 830 for the first time, but it was only USD 1,126, which obviously was $100 off the all-time highs. This recent rally in terms of euros was in the aftermath of concerns over the status of Greece within the Eurozone and discussion of potential contagion: the economies of Spain, Italy, Ireland, and Portugal were most generally mentioned in this respect. This notion of sovereign debt being far from sacrosanct was not the first time that this had happened, but it coming hot on the heels of the financial markets' ructions was another warning to longer-term investors of the advantages of directing a small percentage of their portfolio to the asset that is no one else's debt.

In a resounding emphasis of this, in a presentation to investors on February 25, 2010, JPMorgan Chase & Co.'s chief executive, Jamie Dimon, was widely reported as saying that 200 banks could collapse over the next two years. He also noted that the bank had set limits on its lending to sovereigns (countries) and it may look to hedge some of that. Dimon was also reported as saying that he was more concerned about California's fiscal solvency than about Greece's problems should the state have difficulty in servicing its debt.

I said "longer-term investors" above advisedly because despite the obvious benefits of gold in such a situation, the knee-jerk reaction of markets has often been to sell everything as a "risk" asset—including gold—while retreating to the safety of the U.S. dollar. Consequently, the first move in gold has been lower in such a situation before it climbs once more as investors reappraise their gold and hence gold's superior performance against the euro. (California's particular issues had not really permeated markets at the time of this writing whereas those of Greece had.)

However, we are still a ways off from the inflation-adjusted all-time high, which, depending on whom you talk to and which measure of inflation they use, is generally pitched at around $2,150.

2

What Drives the Price of Gold?

·◦] The Dollar [◦·

To elaborate on the previous chapter: given that gold is quoted in dollars and primarily bought by non-dollar-domiciled individuals, then its price will tend to go up as the U.S. dollar falls. The assumption is that increased buying will come into the market and thus the price has to rise to maintain equilibrium. In a sense that is the "commodity" explanation for gold price moves. A currency explanation would be that as the U.S dollar rises, the price of gold, by definition, must fall, and clearly vice versa.

An example of recent correlations is shown in Figure 2-1. While generally the correlation is extremely high between gold and the euro (the currency most closely watched to gauge moves in gold), at times it has become nearly 1.00 (or perfectly correlated). Figure 2-2 shows the gold and the euro/U.S. dollar exchange rate tracking one another reasonably closely since 2000.

However, it is Figure 2-1 that is more interesting in many ways. This chart shows that the movements of the two are closely correlated at nearly 0.75; it is not the scale of the move but simply that when either gold or the euro goes up,

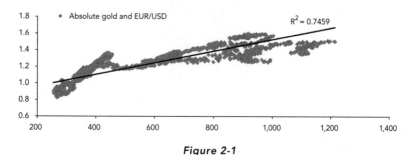

Figure 2-1

Gold and Its Correlation to the EUR/USD Exchange Rate

Source: EcoWin and Barclays Capital

Figure 2-2

The Absolute USD Gold Price and the

EUR/USD Exchange Rate

Source: EcoWin and Barclays Capital

so does the other one. To a purist this comparison might look to be nonsensical since both are quoted against the U.S. dollar. However, I believe it simply shows that gold's overriding driver is the U.S. dollar, and it is this relationship that traders spend the vast majority of their time watching. When traders are bullish for gold and the euro-to-dollar exchange rate is rising, then gold will probably go up by a greater percentage; when traders are more skeptical, gold will go up but by a smaller percentage.

Per my earlier comments, this is not to say that gold exclusively follows the U.S. dollar. For a truer evaluation, it is vital to view its record against other currencies (typically the euro), which should give a clearer picture of the metal's performance and market sentiment.

Indeed, for a clearer restatement of this, the chart in Figure 2-3 has both the U.S. dollar gold price and the euro/U.S. dollar exchange rate tracking each other in the early years of this millennium (the rates have been indexed to 100 for January 2000) and then moving progressively further away as the decade progresses and the gold price rallies against all currencies.

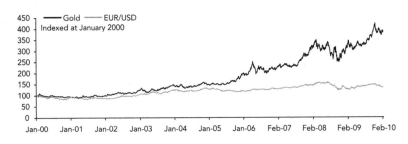

Figure 2-3

Indexed Relationship between Gold and EUR/USD Exchange Rate

Source: EcoWin and Barclays Capital

For those new to the gold market: it does not operate in the same way as a standard commodity market or even like platinum. With other metals, it is much more a case of supply and demand. For example, if a platinum smelter should be forced to close down because of problems, then prices will rise. Indeed, concerns over the power supply to South Africa's platinum mines and smelters caused the metal to rally by over $700 in just one month in early 2008, a rise of some 45 percent.

While gold did move slightly higher in response to the same news, it was much more restrained. First and foremost, South Africa is not responsible for 80 percent of the world's gold supply, while it is the supplier for roughly this amount of the global primary supply of platinum (in the form of mined metal). It is no longer even the world's largest gold producer; according to GFMS, that honor belongs to China. Second, while there are no known large stockpiles of platinum, there are plenty for gold—in effect, the reserves of the central banks or even Asian scrap, which can come onto the market at times when the price is high. Therefore, gold rarely, if ever, trades in accordance with usual supply-and-demand trends—imports falling in one country or rising in another—perhaps with an additional caveat, at least not for very long.

However, the market does look at big-picture supply and demand—that is, the large accumulation or disposal of gold by central banks or the hedging intentions of gold mining companies.

So the market tends to ignore news headlines that Indian gold demand has moved higher or lower, and it will look to other stories on which to base its trading decisions. It is this characteristic of ignoring run-of-the-mill flows of metal that sets gold aside from other commodities and gives it its status as a quasi-currency.

Undoubtedly though, the currency component is the most important long-term factor influencing gold prices. While inflation fears or changes in geopolitics may cause gold to under- or overperform against a variety of currencies, in the end it is the currency component that traders most often refer back to even if it is via a secondary route, that is, gold might temporarily be very closely related to oil, which in turn might be heavily correlated to the U.S. dollar.

·◦[Investment Demand]◦··

The last few years have seen the emergence of commodities as an asset class. More banks have become market makers in this field, or even just white-labeling transactions (marketing products developed by another institution on their behalf under their own brand name), and there has been a rapid rise in the number of institutions offering commodity-linked products to their customers—be they "real money" (pension funds) or leveraged investments (hedge funds and the like).

While gold shares some characteristics with commodities, it has often been included as part of the general argument for diversification, which has been central to the appeal of commodities as an asset class. So while gold is a quasi-currency, it is also a quasi-commodity. However, one of the features that usually makes commodities particularly attractive for long-dated investment is that they have traditionally been backwardated (the forward price is lower than the nearby one), which is very different from the contango market (the forward price is higher than the nearby one) that generally prevails for gold.

Backwardation allows for very attractive trade optics—the term used to describe how a trade looks to the eye without number crunching. For example, if the price of spot gold today is $1,100 and you are told that you can buy it for delivery in two years' time for $1,127, then that does not sound nearly as attractive as being told you can buy three-month copper (the standard delivery time) for $6,870, yet you only have to pay $6,820 if you are prepared to wait two years—the forward price of copper being lower than the nearby price. However, both are fair market prices. This scenario also means that the plethora of investment products that have been offered in commodities have tended to use backwardated commodities wherever possible and have not used gold, particularly where the general outlook is bullish as the optics look far more attractive.

Gold has not been ignored, however, as the psychological affinity that people have for it has led to its inclusion, by demand, in many structured products. This situation simply would not exist for other metals such as zinc or lead.

It is the rise of the exchange-traded funds (ETFs) that probably best demonstrates how dramatically investment interest for gold has changed the landscape. Indeed, across the various gold ETFs there is now some $71 billion invested—a large number, except when compared to estimated total global wealth of some $150 trillion. In other words, the money in ETFs is equivalent to just some 5 basis points of this $150 trillion figure. Even if all other forms of gold holdings are included, this percentage does not creep above 1 percent.

⊰ Physical Demand versus Investment Demand ⊱

While headlines on supply and demand, particularly as related to gold imports or consumption figures, do not generally instantly affect gold prices, physical demand has been the bedrock of the gold market for centuries.

Although it may appear as jewelry rather than investment in bars—simply because different tax structures may make it more sensible to sell the metal as an adornment rather than as a lump—historically this is where most gold was destined to end up. Traditionally it was seen as some 70 percent or so of total supply, but it has now fallen to just over 40 percent.

Indeed, according to figures produced by GFMS, world jewelry fabrication was 1,687 tonnes in 2009. This was a 21-year low; GFMS noted in its publication Gold Survey 2009 Update II, "Not only was the total almost half the 1997 peak of 3,294 tonnes but the fall was the largest absolute decline in GFMS' series." The change in emphasis for gold demand is easily detected in identifiable investment, which GFMS sees as 1,375 tonnes in 2009, up from just 165 tonnes in 2000.

Understandably, with gold prices at record highs, the newswires have been full of headlines such as these from Reuters: "India gold demand falls as prices stay firm," or "Italy jewelry Q1 gold demand down 30 percent," or "Turkish gold jewelry demand seen falling 20 percent." The concern from some quarters is naturally how much has this important sector been alienated from gold over the longer term if some 70 percent or so of gold historically has been destined to become jewelry? The recent high prices have discouraged buying from these traditional sources, and that percentage has dropped to just 45 percent (according to some analysts). Assuming that industrial demand (electronic and dentistry) accounts for some 30 percent, then investment demand needs to account for a minimum of 25 percent of primary supply (newly mined gold) each year or in excess of 600 tonnes. The concern for some is whether the current demand destruction in the metal's traditional jewelry markets will continue and perhaps more importantly whether demand will return if gold prices fall. Or has the substitution effect (smaller and lower-carat pieces or increasingly gem-set) become ingrained?

Given the sentiment in the market, it has been extremely easy for traders to shrug off these stories—a classic case of ignoring bad news. However, they have generally been able to take comfort from the inflow of gold into the various ETFs (covered in more depth in Chapter 7).

While analysts may try to follow the large number of these gold pools around the world, traders really care only about SPDR Gold Shares (previously called streetTRACKS), unless someone prods them to point out a big move in Johannesburg or wherever. Even then, since the flows come out only after the markets have closed, a big move is seen more as an indicator of investor sentiment, particularly because the data are generally three days in arrears.

However, where traditional investment demand is key is in accounting for physical offtake. These markets may suffer in the high-price environment—indeed, even seeing scrap selling rather than just a slowdown in buying—but as long as the decline in this market is offset by the interest in the ETFs, gold can be propelled to new highs, even without the assistance of one of its traditional mainstays. In other words, investment demand replaces physical demand.

Indeed, as mentioned above, a recent refrain has been the notion of just how small the gold market is to global wealth. Based on even the most generous figures, the investable and accessible stocks of the metal rarely account for more than 1 percent of total global wealth. With continuing concern over the state of the world's financial system, if more investment dollars are to chase a fixed supply of the metal, then the price will continue to move higher as cash seeks out a safe haven. After all, unlike money, inflating supply in gold means digging a new mine!

·=| Central Banks |=··

It has been received market wisdom for many years that central banks are buying gold. If they are not actually buying gold, then they are developing strategies. If they are not developing strategies, it will only be a matter of time until they do. Indeed, I have been told by portfolio managers at hedge funds that they "know for a fact that the Fed has ordered China to buy gold." The rationale back in 2005 was that the Fed was trying to hike long-term rates but could not effectively do so when China was buying enormous quantities of U.S. government bonds; therefore, the Chinese were supposedly being told that instead of buying U.S. paper, they had to buy gold. The fact that the math was not even vaguely equivalent didn't matter; perception was all important. However, such is the sensitivity now over how "foreigners" view the currency of the United States that the suggestion that nations are moving away from the currency and into gold, for example, would be enough to send the U.S. dollar lower. Indeed, it is precisely this that is sometimes cited as being behind China's recent decision not to buy gold directly from the International Monetary Fund—China's apparent rejection of the U.S. dollar leading to a plunge in its value and so debasing the value of its foreign currency reserves.

It often seems that commentators compete with each other to release the most sensational claim to enhance their profile and to guarantee press coverage. A particular example I remember is reading on a newswire that an analyst was claiming that a particular oil-producing nation was certain to buy gold; I dismissed it as nonsense, but the market rallied. Why did I take such a high-handed attitude? Simple: the central bank of the country in question was selling gold to me at the time! All of which proves that it is not necessarily the particular properties or outlook for gold that is important but merely sentiment that can drive the price.

Until lately, the 20-year record of central banks in the gold market has been overwhelmingly that of sellers. While the buyers were China, Argentina, Poland (and latterly India, Russia, Sri Lanka, and

Mauritius) and there was some minimal peripheral interest in certain countries where there is a domestic mining industry (such as the Philippines), the list of sellers has been far longer. The United Kingdom, Australia, Switzerland, Norway, France, the Netherlands, Belgium, Austria, the United Arab Emirates, Sweden, Canada, and Portugal have all been sellers of gold. And this list is far from exhaustive.

Admittedly this list of sellers is fairly Euro-centric, but they are also the nations with generally the largest gold holdings and largest percentage of metal in their reserves. During the 1990s the central banks were uniformly seen as sellers, particularly after Australia, Switzerland, and the United Kingdom had all announced plans to dispose of gold. However, the European central bank Gold Agreement took this uncertainty away and was successful to such an extent that this activity is no longer regarded as an overhang. Indeed, the market views central bank selling of 400 tonnes under the current accord (having peaked at 500 tonnes) as being contained in the gold price, and it is more interested if there are shortfalls to this number—that is, if that number is not reached, then it is seen as a bullish signal.

In recent years, despite all the conjecture and rumors to the contrary, the only central banks that have increased their reserves of gold in any meaningful amount, prior to late 2009, were China and Russia. In both instances the increase was assumed to be from domestic production. However, it was the gold purchase by the Reserve Bank of India—more on this later—announced in November 2009 that caught the attention of the market and sparked a great deal of soul-searching about which other institutions would buy and the efficacy of gold as a diversifier or "insurance policy" within a portfolio. More on the activities of the central banks in Chapter 3.

·≈[Diversification and Gold]≈·

The search for diversification and yield has seen hedge funds, pension funds, private banks, sovereign wealth funds, and others all become involved in commodity markets. The assumption from many commentators has been that central banks are also closely involved in this hunt and therefore will turn to the (quasi) commodity that they know best—gold.

The purchase of 31.5 million shares of SPDR ETF gold (equivalent to nearly 100 tonnes of metal and valued at some $3.46 billion at the time of this writing) by John Paulson's Paulson & Co. hedge fund received wide publicity as did the launching of a separate fund dedicated entirely to gold reportedly seeded by $250 million of his own money. However, considerably less publicity was given to Mike Avery, president and chief investment officer of Waddell & Reed Financial, Inc., of Kansas City who, in an article in the *Wall Street Journal* on October 26, 2009, stated that about 15 percent of the $22 billion Asset Strategy funds were then in gold. On the basis of prices prevailing at that time, this would also have given Waddell & Reed a position of roughly 100 tonnes of gold.

As Avery has noted separately, gold has been a currency since the time of King Croesus (roughly 550 BC), and it has a long recognized intrinsic value that is never appreciated more than when countries resort to problem solving by running the printing presses at full steam. Waddell and its clients are concerned that government can default by devaluing its fiat currency, and it is aware that global monetary policy designed to motivate real output has limited effectiveness and, perhaps, this time, won't work. For Waddell owning gold is not about having exposure to mining stocks, futures, or even ETFs. It is about having direct physical access to the underlying bars themselves. While this could be achieved by holding gold in London, Avery determined that his clients would be far better served by having the metal on U.S. soil. While this may seem unusual in some respects, it is not particularly, and steps have been taken to ensure that this metal holding is liquid and can be sold when circumstances warrant.

Similarly, when the Teacher Retirement System of Texas (TRS) announced on October 2, 2009, that "it has launched its first internally managed gold fund with $250 million in assets invested in precious metals mining stocks and exchange-traded funds (ETFs)," this also attracted little comment. Perhaps the media believed that an allocation of $250 million to gold was not particularly noteworthy, or, since TRS has some $100 billion in assets under management, that a small allocation was not particularly relevant.

However, I understand that this is the first time that a U.S. pension fund has launched a separate gold strategy—rather than a commodities strategy. In other words, this is the first time that a pension fund has differentiated gold from other commodities.

Therefore, in both instances commentators should have been much more animated than they were. While Waddell & Reed's investment is reasonably large and TRS's might be seen as fairly small for such a large organization, the fact is that both organizations believed that it was important to diversify into gold. I have picked just companies that have chosen to make their purchases public—there are many more that have opted not to.

While purchases by nations make great headlines and can provoke prolonged bouts of soul-searching from the media, it is instead the myriad lower-profile organizations choosing to invest in gold that are key to its future.

·᠊᠊᠊᠁[Sentiment]᠁᠊᠊·

All markets are sentiment driven, at least partly. Anyone who has ever invested or traded will remember times when *every* piece of bad news was studiously ignored and each piece of good news was seized on as though it were etched in stone, until the time that this swings around by 180 degrees!

Gold reacts exactly in this way: in the late 1990s it was virtually impossible to find anyone who had a positive word to say about it; by 2007 it was the doomsayers who were in short supply. It is this type of trading activity that has sometimes led to gold being described as a postrationalization market. People buy it because they want to—they are not actually sure of the reason or at least cannot point to a single event that spurred them to it. Instead, they buy it first and worry about the rationale later.

I remember having a conversation with the representative of a central bank as to why gold was rallying. He confidently told me that another bank had informed him that the Chinese yuan would be revalued that weekend, and hence the local population was buying gold in anticipation of this. Once the rumor hit the international markets, then professional investors were getting involved too.

Is this situation plausible? At first glance, without thinking about it, probably "yes." However, upon short reflection, you realize that the answer is actually "no." In fact, I pointed out that it was exactly the wrong way to look at it. If the Chinese believed that their currency was being revalued, it would mean fewer yuan per dollar. Therefore, the price of any dollar-denominated asset, such as gold, would actually go down in local currency terms.

However, what was true was that market sentiment was positive, people wanted to buy, and they needed a story to postrationalize their decision. This story seemed to fit in well and hence made the market feel comfortable with its decision. Just for the record, the yuan was not revalued that weekend. Although this is a true story, it is an extreme example. However, the notion of sentiment as a driver of direction is key.

·⊰| Miners |⊱·

Gold producers are still clearly sellers of gold. It is just that they have changed their methodology. For much of the 1990s, banks' precious metal trading desks were mainly focused on servicing the needs of this sector, which, in many instances, involved selling production from future years.

Demands from the miners' shareholders have almost totally ended this as an activity. This in turn has improved sentiment, which has obviated the need for forward selling to a large extent anyway. Indeed, probably the main business that the banks are competing for with this sector is to provide the producers with assistance, or clever structures, in unwinding the existing hedges. This move has been so pronounced that companies that were a key component of global supply became an important element of demand for a while. With almost all of the hedge books now unwound, most of their business currently involves selling their annual production, often just for spot value and at its most basic on a daily basis (that is, in some instances the risk management is little more than digging it out of the ground and selling it).

Indeed, the reduction in the global hedge book has been dramatic, and it is well illustrated by data compiled by Virtual Metals, which they saw as peaking at 102.8 million ounces (3,198 tonnes) in the first quarter of 2001 but which has now dropped to 7.9 million ounces (245 tonnes) as of the end of 2009.

·≈[Inflation]≈·

As a whole, low interest rate environments are positive for gold, and indeed for almost all investments. The logic is simple. If there is a 10 percent interest rate and gold is trading at $1,000, then gold needs to move up a guaranteed $100 over the course of a year to yield as much as the risk-free alternative—such as placing money on deposit or in T-bills. Clearly no free market can offer a guaranteed return, and thus the anticipation has to be for a much greater move. Alternatively, if the interest rate is merely 1 percent, then an investment becomes more compelling and particularly if real interest rates are negative. In the recent environment, the prevalence of all but zero rates of interest for many investors would have stimulated their interest to look at alternative vehicles—in a number of instances, this would have meant gold.

In the 1990s the world seemed as though it was blessed with the "Goldilocks' scenario" of global economic growth while price increases were contained. Clearly the central bankers were doing an excellent job. Inflation was not seen as a threat as the monetary authorities would simply raise rates to contain the problem and ensure that there was little disruption to the economic nirvana. This is the point where the picture diverges sharply from gold's previous nominal high where inflation had been rampant.

That was until August 2007, the point at which "credit crunch" and "subprime crisis" entered the everyday lexicon. While Mervyn King, governor of the Bank of England, initially talked about the "moral hazard" of bailing out institutions whose own policies had been responsible for the difficulties in which they now found themselves, there was little such hesitation elsewhere, with "Ben Bernanke's helicopter" becoming a popular image—cue cartoons of the chairman of the Federal Reserve dropping huge piles of cash on a grateful population.

This divergence was also a result of the different mandates in various countries. Some central banks are charged with maintaining the well-being of the economy as a whole, while others are charged simply with keeping inflation under control. For the former group the situation seemed reasonably clear: it was a trade-off between recession and inflation. The policy was to reduce rates rapidly to stave off a crash in the housing market and to try to avert the knock-on effects, which were seen as far more immediately damaging to the country than inflation. Besides, as previously noted, inflation is seen as containable whereas deflation is not. Countries in the latter group were rather more hamstrung, and instead, the various governments looked at other policies to keep the economy afloat.

Whatever the rationale though, it looked to many as though the monetary authorities were no longer omnipotent. Indeed, they were as much caught up in events that they had as little or no control over as the rest of us.

The result of this turmoil was twofold. First, inflation became a real concern in the major Western economies for the first time in many years, and most importantly in the United States. Second, there was much less trust in the system and the ability of the authorities to control events.

This environment leads to the last of the reasons for gold's rise.

Trust Me: I'm a Banker!

In India roughly two-thirds of the gold that is bought is by the rural, rather than urban, economy. The inference must be that it is unlikely that the country's rich elite live in these villages and that the gold is bought as a form of savings, in particular because the community is uncertain about the security of leaving money in banks either through lack of education or because some institutions have indeed lost their depositors' money or are seen as untrustworthy. Indeed, it is estimated that 15,000 to 20,000 tonnes of gold is held in India.

With the major financial centers seemingly blessed by strong regulation and well-run institutions, the lure of gold in developed countries could be seen as considerably diminished. However, the recent slew of headlines in the press regarding the enormous write-downs that a large number of banks have had to make, and most dramatically the sales of Lehman Brothers to Barclays Bank, of Merrill Lynch to Bank of America, and of Bear Stearns to JPMorgan Chase jolted many out of their complacency.

There is no doubt that faith in the global financial system was damaged. Not only for the general population but, at the time, within the industry itself; the credit crunch being made worse by institutions being unwilling to lend to each other as they were simply not confident in the financial well-being of the borrowers. So when in doubt, keep your cash on hand.

The other aspect about gold is that it is reassuringly straightforward. In a situation where banks were accused of "marking to myth" rather than "marking to market," an investment whose value is readily checkable (and salable) is something of a comfort. Indeed, some of the early motivation behind commodity investments was the purity of the story, supply bottlenecks, and growing demand from China and others. It is a story that can easily be understood without an inordinate number of assumptions. Gold clearly benefited from this desire for simplicity in the early days of its rally, and this trend accelerated once the scale of the problems in financial systems became clear. Or perhaps a truer description might be that since much of the press has been calling for more clarity, it was uncertainty elsewhere that saw gold breach $1,000 for the first time.

In such a situation it is comforting to have an investment that is not anyone else's obligation. In other words, this was an environment tailor-made to boost interest in gold.

·≺[Conclusion]≻·

So it was not any one feature that drove the gold price and took it to record levels, and not just against the U.S. dollar but against the euro, the pound, the Swiss franc, and others. Instead, it was a number of issues that came together to propel the market higher. While the importance of these various factors will fluctuate, there is little doubt that the current economic and investing environment has rekindled interest in gold for many reasons, something that is unlikely to change suddenly.

3

The Official Sector

·◦[The Perception of Gold]◦·

A quick read of the media has probably assured most people not intimately acquainted with the gold market that central banks are keen buyers of the metal. Indeed, much is being made of the fact that gold is the third "currency" behind the U.S. dollar and the euro, and therefore these institutions need the metal as a constituent of their reserves: an essential part of any portfolio.

A quick roundup of some fairly recent remarks highlights this trend: "If we were the governor of the People's Bank of China or Reserve Bank of India or the Bank of Japan, we know what we would be doing: we would be quietly, but consistently, putting EUR and Dollar reserves on the offer and we would be, quietly and consistently, on the bid for gold." Thus wrote Dennis Gartman of the eponymous and influential newsletter in November 2005. Indeed, this has been a recurrent theme of his and that of many other commentators.

In some instances the central banks have also been entering the debate. Consider the following: "China should appropriately increase its gold reserves and buy more oil, metals and other strategic materials so as to broaden the investment channels of the foreign exchange reserves." The media reported these remarks as being made by Xiang Junbo, one of the deputy governors of the People's Bank of China (China's central bank). In 2009 a local official was apparently quoted as saying that China should increase its gold reserves to 5,000 tonnes within three years (up from the current 1,054 tonnes) and to 10,000 tonnes within five years. This story was recounted to me by a local mining company executive exasperated at some of the outlandish statements that hit the newswires from time to time. To achieve these targets, China would need to buy almost the entire world's annual production every year—clearly impossible.

The Russians probably elicited the most excitement when Maria Gueguina, then head of foreign exchange reserve management at that country's central bank, said in a speech to the London Bullion Market Association (LBMA) gold conference in Johannesburg (November 2005) that "calculations of the Central Bank of Russia . . . showed that about 10 percent of gold in reserves would be appropriate with regard for special requirements." Although Gueguina subsequently clarified her remarks as being "theoretical," the price rallied strongly and particularly in the following few days as the same question was asked of other senior officials. The chairman of the central bank was quoted as saying that the gold "question is being discussed," and Reuters reported that then "Russian President Vladimir Putin threw his weight behind the idea of boosting the share of gold in the central bank's fast-growing reserves."

At the time the Russians held 438 tonnes of gold, and the metal made up just 2.5 percent of the total reserves. In the interim these figures have moved up to 4.7 percent and 607.7 tonnes. To get to 10 percent would require the Russians to more than double their reserves and to buy a further 685 tonnes (21.9 million ounces). Despite this jump in their reserves, there has been scant evidence of large quantities of gold being bought from the market—or other nations—although over the last two years, they have moved from the world's eleventh largest holder to the tenth.

Generally though, it does not need a statement for analysts to speculate as to which country might be buying gold. All it needs is rapidly growing foreign exchange reserves and perhaps a poor relationship with the United States. The latter is often viewed as a requirement because it is assumed that these countries do not want to hold large quantities of dollars. Thus some of the countries that have been cited as buyers of gold, as they fit into at least one of the categories, are Saudi Arabia, Russia, India, Iran, Venezuela, South Africa, and Brazil.

·◦] Holders of Gold [◦·

The world's current largest holders of the metal, and the percentage it constitutes of their reserves, are shown in Table 3-1 (data as of December 2009). A realistic appraisal of these figures shows that the world's largest holders of gold, certainly in percentage terms, are the

Table 3-1

World's Largest Holders of Gold

GLOBAL RANKING	COUNTRY	GOLD HOLDINGS (TONNES)	PERCENT RESERVES
1	United States	8,133.5	68.7%
2	Germany	3,407.6	64.6%
3	IMF	3,005.3	—
4	Italy	2,451.8	63.4%
5	France	2,435.4	64.2%
6	China	1,054.4	1.5%
7	Switzerland	1,040.1	28.8%
8	Japan	765.2	2.5%
9	Netherlands	612.5	51.7%
10	Russia	607.7	4.7%
11	India	557.7	6.4%

Source: © World Gold Council and International Monetary Fund.

"old economies" of the West with Asia represented by only China, Japan, and latterly India (hence my decision to show the top 11 rather than the top 10 largest holders). However, their metal holdings are just tiny percentages of their overall reserves.

Taking a look at the Asian economies themselves as shown in Table 3-2, it is clear just how little gold some of these institutions hold both as a percentage and simply numerically. So while the Asian nations listed in Table 3-2, on average, hold around 3.5 percent of their reserves in gold (removing the outliers of Sri Lanka and Hong Kong), the figure for the European countries (Table 3-3) is generally over 50 percent and in the case of Portugal, markedly so.

Table 3-2
Leading Asian Holders of Gold

WORLDWIDE RANKING	COUNTRY	GOLD HOLDINGS (TONNES)	PERCENT RESERVES
6	China	1,054.0	1.5%
8	Japan	765.2	2.4%
11	India	557.7	6.4%
13	Taiwan	423.6	4.1%
22	Philippines	154.7	12.1%
25	Singapore	127.7	2.3%
33	Thailand	84.0	2.1%
38	Indonesia	73.1	3.9%
45	Malaysia	36.4	1.3%
56	Sri Lanka	15.3	22.3%
57	Korea	14.4	0.2%
86	Hong Kong	2.0	0%

Source: © World Gold Council and International Monetary Fund.

Table 3-3
Leading Western Holders of Gold

WORLDWIDE RANKING	COUNTRY	GOLD HOLDINGS (TONNES)	PERCENT RESERVES
1	United States	8,133.5	68.7%
2	Germany	3,407.6	64.6%
4	Italy	2,451.8	63.4%
5	France	2,435.4	64.2%
7	Switzerland	1,040.1	28.8%
9	Netherlands	612.5	51.7%
12	European Central Bank	501.4	19.6%
14	Portugal	382.5	83.8%
16	United Kingdom	310.3	15.2%
18	Spain	281.6	34.6%
19	Austria	280.0	52.7%
20	Belgium	227.5	31.8%

Source: © World Gold Council and International Monetary Fund.

Looking back on the statistics for movements in central bank gold holdings over the last 10 years, there is a preponderance of minus signs. In other words, sales of gold are the dominant feature of central banks' activity in the gold market and particularly in the earlier part of this period. True, there were some purchases, but these tended to be relatively modest and often stemmed from a requirement that small-scale domestic miners have to sell the metal to the central bank, which can either add the gold to its reserves or sell it into the international market.

Until recently the only headline grabbers were the purchase by Poland of gold in the 1990s—assumed to have been bought from another European central bank—as well as the announcements by China that it had bought metal in 2002 and 2003, and finally the statement by Argentina in 2004 that it had purchased slightly under 30 tonnes of metal for reserve diversification.

A little bit of history: In January 2002, China announced an increase in its gold reserves from 12.7 to 16.08 million ounces. The original figure, released to the International Monetary Fund (IMF) for the first time in the 1970s, had been unchanged until the press release. This increase in 2002 occurred despite a long-standing law mandating the sale of the country's gold production to the central bank (People's Bank of China, also known as the PBoC). The PBoC then adjusted the domestic price to allow gold to flow into, or out of, the country. Almost exactly a year later, the figure rose again to 19.29 million ounces, or roughly 602 tonnes. The reaction at the time was subdued as analysts assumed that rather than being fresh purchases of the metal, the increases were more a restatement of balances actually held.

Indeed, the figures reported to the IMF are not independently audited, and thus there have been suggestions of both over- and underreporting by a number of countries.

More recently we have seen a series of eye-catching announcements. First of all was the statement from China in April 2009 that its gold reserves had increased by 454 tonnes to 1,054 tonnes. It seems that the metal had been accumulated since 2003 and was possibly a combination of scrap and domestic production. Apparently the reason news of the increase had been released at this time was that the refining process had only just been completed.

In November 2009, there were the purchases by India, Sri Lanka, and Mauritius from the IMF. This started off a bout of speculation as to who would buy the remainder of the gold that the IMF was offering for sale—with China generally touted as the favorite. However, at the time of this writing, these three confirmed purchases accounted for 212 tonnes (200, 10, and 2 tonnes, respectively), and there is as yet no sign of any other country looking to buy the remaining metal.

Given the enormous size of China's international reserves (some $2.4 trillion), the meager percentage taken up by gold (1.5 percent), and the populace's cultural affinity for gold, many commentators declared that China was to buy the gold that the IMF had to sell. The only real debates from some quarters were that China wanted to pay some notional historic price, or buy only 50 tonnes rather than 200, and so on. While this may have been true, I frankly doubt it. The numbers were simply too small for extended debate to have taken up so much of the time of the country's leaders. Instead, I believe that the decision as to whether or not to buy the offered gold was rather more simplistic:

> **Alternative 1:** "China should buy the gold to send a strong message to President Obama's administration that it disagrees with the apparent current policy of dollar depreciation."

> **Alternative 2:** "China cannot buy the gold from the IMF as this would signal to financial markets our displeasure with the policies of President Obama's administration and the potential for a longer-term move toward investments other than the U.S. dollar, which would include gold. Such an interpretation would cause further currency weakness and thus negatively impact the overall value of China's foreign currency reserves."

I believe that it is the latter view which won out. Unless any other country comes forward, then the IMF will sell the gold on the open market. Indeed, the IMF made such an announcement on February 17, 2010, which caused a $20 drop in the gold price—although the IMF has said that it is still looking for purchasers. This sell-off in gold was apparently sparked by some analysts decrying that since the IMF was able to dispose of only half its proposed tonnage, then this spelled an end to central bank interest in the gold market.

There may be some truth in this. However, I think that it owes rather more to the fact that the publicity that these purchases would garner may be rather more than some countries would wish for. I imagine there are some institutions that, on hearing that the Reserve Bank of India had paid some $1,045 for its gold, were imagining the reactions of their domestic media and politicians if their purchase price was similarly revealed. And they were imagining the opportunities for point scoring should the price slip below that paid. Perhaps an inquiry calling into question the probity of the central bank governor and the board?—a situation no civil servants would want to expose themselves to. Sovereign wealth funds (SWFs) by and large shun the limelight, and for them to have their latest acquisition all over the newswires would not have been attractive.

Ultimately this means that it is indeed likely that the IMF will sell its remaining 191.3 tonnes of gold on the open market as no other nations may come forward to buy. If the IMF is forced to sell gold directly to the markets—rather than to countries—I firmly believe that these sales will be carried out in small amounts over an extended period of time rather than through auctions, which were favored by the IMF in the 1970s and the U.K. government over the turn of the millennium.

However, it is worth not losing sight of the fact that it seems inevitable that both China and Russia will continue to accumulate gold from domestic production. While this does not grab as many headlines, it does remove gold from the market, and it has the advantage for the buyer that it is difficult to judge the price paid. Indeed, on March 3, 2010, First Deputy Chairman Ulyukaev of the Central Bank of Russia was quoted on the newswires as saying that the central bank was prepared to buy all the gold produced by the country's mining industry as long as it did not disrupt markets. Clearly there are always going to be some nuances missed in a translation, but currently Russia produces roughly 100 tonnes of gold each year more than the central bank buys. However, there was no clarity as to how much the domestic market consumes and exactly how relevant it was. Although it must be regarded as an encouraging statement of intent, and it seems likely that little, if any, gold produced in Russia will find its way onto the international markets.

Additionally, many of the countries that might have been assumed to be sellers have lost that particular appetite in recent years as the gold price has soared. However, some of those nations holding almost all their reserves in precious metal may be obligated to sell even if only in the interests of restoring balance.

⋅◦[Buyers of Gold?]◦⋅

Before asking which other countries might buy gold, it is worth examining why a central bank should hold gold in the first place. The standard answer would then lead to debate on diversification, gold being no one's debt, and an impression of tradition and solidity: the standard features attributed to gold.

Assuming that the diversification argument is generally the strongest, many central banks will classify their mission as the preservation of reserves by ensuring liquidity, a basically conservative approach. Central banks tend not to be wealth creators but rather are charged with maintaining a status quo—something that can be seen both as part of their charter as well as reflected in their remuneration, in which performance incentive payments are relatively rare. In this sense gold fits the requirements well. It is a traditional asset and one held by the majority of central banks.

Assuming that China, Russia, and India—countries that have been acquiring gold—decided to purchase more metal for diversification, then how much metal would this involve? A 1 percent holding of gold is clearly too little to count; the most recent large central bank to be inaugurated was the European Central Bank, which opted for 15 percent, although this amount is more related to the fact that the bank's members were almost all large holders of the metal in the first place, over 50 percent in some cases. So perhaps a figure of 10 percent might be appropriate (Table 3-4), particularly given the theoretical remarks by Maria Gueguina of the Central Bank of Russia. This figure also has the advantage of being slightly over double the 3 to 5 percent that many institutions are seeking to invest in commodity markets: a new asset class rather than a traditional central bank staple.

Table 3-4
Theoretical Gold Purchases by the Central Banks of China, Russia, and India

COUNTRY	10 PERCENT GOLD HOLDINGS	CURRENT RESERVES	REQUIRED PURCHASE
China	7,026.6t	1,054.0t	5,972.6t
Russia	1,293.0t	607.7t	685.3t
India	871.4t	557.7t	313.7t

Note: t = tonnes

By this very rough measure, for just these three institutions to hold 10 percent of their reserves in gold, they would have to purchase 6,971.6 tonnes. This is equivalent to over 2½ years of global gold production. To put this into perspective, under the selling agreement reached by the European central banks, the signatories are limited to selling 400 tonnes of gold between them per annum—this figure being seen as a quantity that should not unduly disrupt the market. Adopting the same logic, it would take over 17 years for these three institutions to reach their target, by which time their reserves would doubtless have grown substantially.

When, in early 2008, I originally wrote *Investing in Gold*, the percentage of gold within reserves was considerably lower for both Russia and India. Since that time, the overall amount in their reserves has fluctuated, and both have bought gold. It is now rather more possible that both countries could seek to move toward 10 percent of their reserves in gold as a diversifying factor, but for China this simply remains impossible—both the size of its reserves and the speed at which they are growing count against them. However, there is no doubt that the Chinese will continue to accumulate gold from domestic production—it is, after all, the world's largest producer of gold: a title that it acquired after overtaking South Africa's position for the first time in 2007.

The Official Sector

More generally though, the problem that central banks have had with gold is its high profile. If a central bank opts to increase the percentage of euros it holds in its reserves at the expense of U.S. dollars, then that is a short-lived headline for the financial markets. If this same central bank were to start selling its gold holdings, then this often would presage a press campaign fixated on some form of family heirloom being disposed of in an underhanded way. In 1999, when Gordon Brown was chancellor of the exchequer, the rather bizarre title by which the United Kingdom denotes its minister of finance, he opted to sell 395 tonnes of the country's gold reserves at an approximate average price per tonne of $275—a decision that is still recalled whenever his detractors wish to question his financial competence.

This situation exemplifies the dilemma that gold presents for the official sector: that gold has been a buy-and-hold investment. Once owned, gold is extremely difficult to dispose of. A fitting metaphor is that of the lobster trap—it's very tempting to enter but next to impossible to exit. Nevertheless, I see three possibilities for more state entities to buy significant quantities of gold, the first being in countries like India where there is a cultural affinity to gold and the current percentage of the metal in rapidly expanding reserves is small (so a diversification motive), and the second being in something of an autocratic country where the central bank is instructed to accumulate gold. The third is via SWFs, in which a nation would simply treat the investment as an unannounced trading position—in effect, a radical departure from the sort of activities that we have seen from countries in the past—so that the gold could be sold again at the appropriate time. Current estimates are that the SWFs have some $3 trillion under management, and again even a few percentage points of investment would translate to an enormous investment in this market—each percentage point accounting for over 900 tonnes (on a basis of $1,000 per ounce). The result would be similar if the world's mutual fund, pension, and insurance companies decided to invest in gold. Although quite how they could access sufficient quantities of gold is another question.

Stop the presses! On March 9, 2010, a gentleman by the name of Yi Gang, who is the deputy governor of the PBoC, the head of the State Administration of Foreign Exchange (SAFE), and the overseer of China's reserves, gave a press conference. Barclays Capital reported his remarks as: "On China's purchase of gold, he said that over the past few years, China has increased its official holdings of gold by 400 tons to 1,054 tons, which, in value terms, accounts for less than 2 percent of China's total foreign reserves. Even if China doubles its holdings, gold will not be a major reserve investment. China will also cautiously consider increasing gold reserves, as any large purchases by China would boost gold prices, which would hurt private Chinese buyers. Moreover, he noted that the large price swings in gold over the past 30 years do not seem to have offered a good return on investment."

So, as was suggested earlier, the magnitude of China's reserves and the relatively small size of the gold market make it virtually impossible for China to accumulate a significant proportion of its reserves in gold. However, it certainly does not preclude continued purchases from domestic production.

⋅≺| Central Banks Selling Gold |≻⋅

For much of the 1990s gold was in an unremitting bear market. It was seen as an antiquated investment whose time had passed in favor of a new era of financial engineering and the dot-com boom. Even gold producers were, in many instances, selling gold that they had yet to mine to protect the future of their operations, and speculators were short-selling gold in a version of the yen "carry trade"—essentially where hedge funds and others would sell gold, borrow it back at the low gold interest rate, and then invest the dollars from their sales in high-yielding instruments (or even in Treasury bills). The fact that gold was slipping lower meant that not only were speculators gaining on the yield but they were also enjoying a capital appreciation as the price of the metal kept falling.

The Official Sector

Rightly, many central banks were unwilling to simply watch as gold fell ever lower and the national wealth evaporated. Toward the end of the decade, we saw the Belgians, Dutch, and Canadians, along with other nations, selling gold. The nadir came when, during the course of 1999, a number of nations that were thought to be friendly to the metal sought to lighten up on their holdings.

The Australians had sold in 1997, and in 1999 the United Kingdom and Switzerland both declared their intention to divest roughly half of their holdings; the Swiss divested a rather more material 1,300 tonnes compared to the United Kingdom's 395 tonnes.

The market had, to a certain extent, gotten used to the idea that central banks sell gold. Investors did not care for this idea, but it was accepted. However, when news of the Australian sale broke, the market was caught totally off guard. The fact that the press release seemed to suggest that the Reserve Bank of Australia and the government had decided on this course of action because the country had plenty of metal in the ground did little to satisfy the detractors.

The mining companies were particularly unimpressed and pointed out that the unmined gold belonged to them rather than to the government—adding insult to injury, the announcement caused the gold price to sink further.

In the same way, it was assumed that the Swiss had some sort of affinity for gold, that it was as much a part of their culture as chocolate and banking. However, this was evidently not the case. In a similar fashion, London is generally seen as the home of the gold market, with the majority of metal around the world trading loco London, where the benchmark gold price (the fixing) is determined. Furthermore, it is also home to many of the largest global market makers and the place where the rules defining the industry standard, the "London Good Delivery" bar, are set. The United Kingdom was a long-term holder of gold. In the same way as with the Swiss, the market had been rather too complacent, and the U.K. government, which actually owns the United Kingdom's reserves (unlike the situation in most other countries where it belongs to the central bank), was indeed a seller and preferred to hold the euro.

The unexpected actions of these three countries in particular gave many investors the impression that all central banks were queuing up to sell gold, that it was far more a question of *when* every holder sold rather than *if*. The fact that three countries that had been considered to be "friendly" to gold were all selling gave rise to the suspicion that the outlook was so bearish that countries were leapfrogging each other in their eagerness to divest.

Gold plumbed 19-year lows during 1999, falling to $252, with some mining companies accusing the central banks of not only distorting the gold market by selling but also helping hedge funds—which borrowed gold to fund their carry trades—to push the price lower. The rejoinder from the official sector was simple and to the point: they felt that it was the producers whose hedging policies were to blame, that "accelerated selling" was the real destroyer of value. One memorable rejoinder I heard from a senior central banker was: "At least we are selling gold that we already have; not something that might not even be dug up for 10 years."

On September 26, 1999, the situation changed dramatically.

·≡] European central bank Gold Agreement [≡·

The heading "European central bank Gold Agreement" might look like a weird mixture of upper- and lowercase letters, a typographical error, but the agreement is normally referred to as EcbGA, although sometimes also as WAG, the Washington Agreement on Gold. This jumble of letters was to underline the scope of the agreement while seeking to make clear that this was not simply a declaration by the European Central Bank (thus giving all capitals) but to show that a number of European central banks were involved.

On Monday September 27, 1999, I was working in Sydney. Given the time difference, it was a Sunday and a day earlier in Washington when Wim Duisenberg (the then president of the European Central Bank) issued a statement on behalf of 15 central banks.

These 15 institutions were the central banks of the United Kingdom, Switzerland, Sweden, and the ECB, plus the Euroland

11—namely, Germany, France, Italy, the Netherlands, Portugal, Spain, Austria, Belgium, Luxembourg, Finland, and Ireland.

·⟨ EcbGA–Mark I ⟩·

1. Gold will remain an important element of global monetary reserves.

2. The above institutions will not enter the market as sellers, with the exception of already decided sales.

3. Gold sales already decided will be achieved through a concerted program of sales over the next five years. Annual sales will not exceed approximately 400 tonnes, and total sales over this period will not exceed 2,000 tonnes.

4. The signatories to this agreement have agreed not to expand their gold leasings and their use of gold futures and options over this period.

5. This agreement will be reviewed after five years.

The initial reaction was one of caution. Everyone knew it was important, but what should the gold price do? It had closed on Friday night at around $267 in New York, and from there it started to creep up slowly. Bizarre as it might seem now, much of the market's attention initially focused on the impact to the gold lending market, where there were already concerns over the "Y2K bug" plus liquidity constraints over the turn of the year and the millennium. I called all the clients in my address book and woke people up from Europe to the United States. Again there were few buyers, but everyone wanted to be kept "in touch."

The media had no such reservations. Instead, newswires and newspapers were full of articles trumpeting the restraint of the central banks, despite the fact that the total of 2,000 tonnes to be sold over five years was more than double the sales from these countries over the previous ten years. The result was that gold rallied to $338 over the course of the next few days—a gain of some 26 percent. Gold interest rates soared too, with one-month rates reaching a high of 10 percent from 4 percent just a few days earlier.

As the metal's price started to spike, gold mining companies started to make announcements of their own. One of the first was Ghana's Ashanti Goldfields, which announced that it had restructured 80 percent of its hedge book, converting "forward sale positions into synthetic (put) options." Technically this restructuring would have involved the company buying call options with the same strike and expiry as the existing sales. Clearly this looked to be a smart move until October 5, 1999, when the company announced that the hedge book had a negative value of some $450 million. Subsequently Ashanti announced that it had entered into a standstill agreement with its 16 bank counterparts, which had agreed not to request further margin calls. The company was ultimately taken over by Anglo-Gold in April 2004 to form AngloGold Ashanti.

Similarly, Cambior Inc. of Canada announced that it was in discussions with banks "to determine . . . the manner and sequence in which Cambior's gold delivery obligations will be met."

The fact that the gold price could rally but companies that mine gold might still lose money was not a prospect that had probably ever occurred to investors.

However, just three months later, almost all these gains had been given back—despite the predictions of doom as the world approached New Year's Eve 1999—with spot gold back at $274 and one-month gold deposits paying only 1.5 percent.

The Producers

While governments and their related institutions can enter into agreements to regulate supply, the same leeway cannot be extended to individuals or typical companies. Think of OPEC or indeed the signatories to EcbGA. However, for companies the accusations would be of antitrust and cartels, with the consequent potential for enormous damages from class-action lawsuits. Thus there was no chance that the miners could respond formally, as a group, to the statement from the central banks.

However, in early 2000 a number of press releases were issued by individual producers. All were basically to the effect that they would rein back their hedging, also known as "accelerated supply." In February 2000, Placer Dome (then the third-largest North American gold mining company) announced: "As of this day, the company has ceased adding any new hedge positions" and "We believe that gold prices will move higher. The agreement by European central banks to limit their sales and lending was an important step toward improving market sentiment, but industry needs to do its part."

Ultimately, it was the formal statement by the 15 central banks and the impact that it had on the activities of individual mining companies that allowed the recent rally in gold to all-time highs to take place. Simply put, it removed uncertainty and let positive sentiment flourish.

EcbGA–Mark II

The original agreement was so influential that almost immediately rumors emerged that it would be abrogated. These rumors were rapidly followed by conjecture as to whether it would be renewed. Both of these stories were avidly reported in the financial press, but in my view there was never any question that the central banks would not closely follow the strictures that they themselves had set. Any suggestion that they were "bending the rules" would undoubtedly have impacted the reputation of central banks for many years to come and would have made their lives far harder in markets where it is vital that their pronouncements are taken at face value (interest rate policy, for example).

The rumors were dispelled six months earlier than necessary, on March 8, 2004, when the following statement appeared on the Web site of the ECB (www.ecb.int):

> In the interests of clarifying their intentions with respect to their gold holdings, the undersigned institutions make the following statement:
>
> 1. Gold will remain an important element of global monetary reserves.
>
> 2. The gold sales already decided and yet to be decided by the undersigned institutions will be achieved through a concerted program of sales over a period of five years, starting on September 27, 2004, just after the end of the previous agreement. Annual sales will not exceed 500 tonnes, and total sales over this period will not exceed 2,500 tonnes.
>
> 3. Over this period, the signatories to this agreement have agreed that the total amount of gold leasings and the total amount of their use of gold futures and options will not exceed the amounts prevailing and the date of the signature of the previous agreement.
>
> 4. This agreement will be reviewed after five years.

This time the signatories were the European Central Bank, Banco de España (Spain), Bank of Greece, Banque de France, Central Bank and Financial Services Authority of Ireland, De Nederlandsche Bank (the Netherlands), Oesterreichisch Nationalbank (Austria), Schweizerische Nationalbank (Switzerland), Banca d'Italia (Italy), Banco de Portugal, Banque Nationale de Belgique (Belgium), Deutsche Bundesbank (Germany), Suomen Pankki (Finland), and Sveriges Riksbank (Sweden).

At the time of signing, these institutions had combined gold holdings of approximately 13,900 tonnes, which equated to around 40 percent of all gold then held by the official sector.

Since the announcement was made, the original signatories were joined by the central banks of Slovenia, Malta, and Cyprus. The latter pair was the most recent, signing up on January 25, 2008.

⊰ Mark I versus Mark II ⊱

The most significant change was that the tonnage of sales was increased from 2,000 tonnes over five years up to 2,500 tonnes, an increase in allowable sales of 100 tonnes per annum. The amount was judged by the central banks as one not to cause any market disruption, and it was arrived at after considerable informal consultation with the largest gold trading banks. In all the accords this figure is the maximum amount that can be sold in any quota year (September 27 to September 26) rather than a target. Thus the full year allowable amount does not need to be filled—an important consideration and one that has helped the recent rally in the gold price. Unwritten in the agreement is that the original EcbGA was about returning stability to the gold market. Indeed, I know there was debate, originally and subsequently, about the first tenet that "gold will remain an important element of global monetary reserves"; in many ways, this was an odd remark from institutions that were embarking on selling it, but the message was deemed important to help sentiment.

Therefore, while signatory central banks are allowed to roll any gold sales forward, there has been a conscious effort to ensure that the settlement date of the transactions falls within the relevant quota year. Similarly, these institutions have been involved in the options market, tending to sell call options. These options have generally been assumed to be 100 percent delta—that is, the options are accounted for at full face value until they expire rather than at the values suggested by the option pricing models, again to ensure that they are complying with the spirit of the accord.

While both agreements were originally signed by 15 countries, in Mark II Greece took the place of the Bank of England. The rationale given by the Bank of England for not participating was this: "The U.K. government has no plans to sell holdings of gold from its reserves and will therefore not participate in the renewal of the Agreement on Gold announced by European Central Banks today. The Government remains firmly committed to transparency and ensuring the integrity of the gold market. Consequently an announcement will be made if the U.K.'s policy on gold sales changes in the future."

All perfectly logical, except that cynics pointed out that some other signatories were also extremely unlikely to sell gold as they had such small balances, in particular pointing to Ireland (5.5 tonnes) and Luxembourg (2.3 tonnes). However, the concerns of the conspiracy theorists have not been borne out.

EcbGA–Mark III

If the European central banks intended to adhere to their original timing, then markets should have known by March 2009 whether there was likely to be a further five-year extension. Indeed, I had a number of them ask my opinion as early as March 2008 as to whether another accord was necessary. My perception is that these institutions, in common with all of us, do not like to be restricted and would be far happier to have freedom of action. Therefore, their preference would be merely to note that gold has recently reached all-time nominal highs and therefore there is no need for a further agreement. They could also note that the rationale for the original agreement was to provide stability and certainty to a market beset by rumor and pessimism—in this their original action accomplished its purpose extremely well.

However, at that time, my response to these central banks was that gold is very much a sentiment-driven market. Thus while the current market could probably shrug off the lack of EcbGA Mark III, it would be by no means assured that the same would be true at a later date. Therefore, given that markets generally like certainty, it would be preferable if the accord were to be renewed for a further term. A renewal would be particularly important should the IMF be successful in its quest to sell gold as it ultimately turned out to be.

The Official Sector

In the run-up to March 2009 (five years since the announcement of the rollover of the previous accord), there was a guessing game between the market and the European Central Bank as to when any new agreement would be announced—certainly the ECB remained very tight lipped. When March gave way to April, May, and June, the market began to wonder if there was to be no new agreement at all. Admittedly the central banks had other things to worry about—the global liquidity and credit squeeze, for example. However, on August 7, 2009, the EcbGA Mark III was finally announced. It would follow on directly from the end of the previous deal and start on September 27, 2009. It read:

> In the interest of clarifying their intentions with respect to their gold holdings, the undersigned institutions make the following statement:
>
> 1. Gold remains an important element of global monetary reserves.
>
> 2. The gold sales already decided and to be decided by the undersigned institutions will be achieved through a concerted program of sales over a period of five years, starting on September 27, 2009, immediately after the end of the previous agreement. Annual sales will not exceed 400 tonnes, and total sales over this period will not exceed 2,000 tonnes.
>
> 3. The signatories recognize the intention of the IMF to sell 403 tonnes of gold and noted that such sales can be accommodated within the above ceilings.
>
> 4. This agreement will be reviewed after five years.

This agreement was signed by all signatories to EcbGA Mark II plus Banque centrale du Luxembourg and Národná banka Slovenska (the National Bank of Slovakia).

⤝❙ Mark II versus Mark III ❙⤛

The three key differences in this press release from that of five years earlier are these:

1. The amount of gold that can be sold has been reduced to 2,000 tonnes from 2,500 under the previous agreement. Under EcbGA Mark I the total quota that could be sold was 2,000 tonnes (just to reinforce that this is the maximum and not a target), and all of that was disposed of. When this was renewed, the ceiling was raised to 2,500 tonnes, but in the latter years the 12-month quota maximum was rarely reached.

   Indeed, just 1,884 tonnes were sold over the five years, rather than the allowable 2,500 tonnes (the final two years ran at just 359 and 157 tonnes, respectively, against a quota of 500 tonnes each year). Not exactly indicative of a burning desire to sell from the signatories.

2. The intention of the IMF—which is not a signatory—has been "recognized." Under the current agreement the 2,000 tonnes looks to me to be far more about the length of the agreement than the numbers of sellers. To be rather clearer, I believe that in 1999 the total was reached by adding up the amounts each country wished to sell. By 2009 it had simply become a number with sufficient "wiggle room" to accommodate the IMF and any other country where the circumstances might change between August 2009 and September 2014. For example, would Italy or Greece sell gold to reduce its budgetary deficits? However, whether this would be allowed under EU accounting rules is open to much debate. Or perhaps Germany to fund an educational trust? And so on. Indeed, without the sales from the IMF, it is not easy to identify who the willing sellers might be.

3. Finally the signatories got rid of one tenet that was in the previous two agreements—namely, "Over this period, the

signatories to this agreement have agreed that the total amount of gold leasings and the total amount of their use of gold futures and options will not exceed the amounts prevailing at the date of the signature of the previous agreement." Given the collapse in gold interest rates and the subsequent disinterest from central banks on a risk/reward basis, then this is unlikely to be missed.

The IMF and Gold

Under the charter of the International Monetary Fund, the organization is allowed to hold gold or to sell it. There is no middle ground as there is for most official institutions, which can at least attempt to earn a return by lending their gold. So the gold just sits on their balance sheet and serves very little purpose—particularly as it is at a historic price around $71 per ounce.

The IMF has previously sold gold, through a series of successful auctions during the 1970s. The recent discussions really began in earnest during the late 1990s, when then British prime minister Tony Blair suggested that the IMF sell gold to assist the Heavily Indebted Poor Countries (HIPC—pronounced "hipic"). While this had some support, it was also roundly condemned by the more vociferous. The complaints were generally these:

1. It is not the IMF's gold to dispose of as it wishes; instead, it belongs to the countries that originally granted it to the IMF. Therefore, if the IMF has no further use for its gold, it should simply hand it back to the original donors.

2. The IMF is an inefficient and bureaucratic organization, and it should first get its own finances in order before dispensing largesse.

3. Most tellingly though, several African nations with mining industries lined up to condemn the proposals. They cited increased gold sales as damaging to the very nations that the disposal was supposed to help.

Unsurprisingly, the idea was dropped, although there were a series of one-off "accounting tricks" that allowed the IMF to value some gold at market prices and thus grow its balance sheet. The IMF provides this account on its Web site: "Between December 1999 and April 2000, separate but closely linked transactions involving a total of 12.9 million ounces of gold were carried out between the IMF and two members (Brazil and Mexico) that had financial obligations falling due to the IMF. In the first step, the IMF sold gold to the member at the prevailing market price, and the profits were placed in a special account invested for the benefit of the HIPC Initiative. In the second step, the IMF immediately accepted back, at the same market price, the same amount of gold from the member in settlement of that member's financial obligations. The net effect of these transactions was to leave the balance of the IMF's holdings of physical gold unchanged." (For further details, see www.imf.org/external/np/exr/facts/gold.htm.)

For the market, the situation remained unchanged until January 2007, with the emergence of the Eminent Persons Group's report on gold sales. This time it was clear that the IMF had sought to forestall the type of criticism that it had faced before. Also, the notion of helping the HIPC had been dropped in favor of sales settling the IMF's financing needs.

This report marked a major departure from the political "kite-flying" that we saw previously. This time attempts were made to address the majority of the criticisms that might be leveled at it. Importantly, the persons who actually put their name to the report were of sufficient stature to dispel most doubts that this was a serious proposal.

First, the commission included Tito Mboweni, governor of the South African Reserve Bank. South Africa had been a vocal critic of the original proposals, some 10 years earlier, for the IMF to sell gold, arguing that it would actually harm the Heavily Indebted Poor Countries that it was supposed to help. On subsequent occasions, South Africa toned down its displeasure and aligned with those pro-selling. Indeed, the chairman (Andrew Crockett formerly of the Bank for International Settlements but by then president of JPMorgan Chase

International) went out of his way at a press conference to emphasize that South Africa was part of the group and that the committee "has been quite careful to try to devise proposals that do not create dangers of destabilizing the gold market." (See further at www.imf.org/exter nal/np/tr/2007/tr070131.htm.)

Also present in the Eminent Persons Group was Jean-Claude Trichet. As president of the ECB, he would obviously be able to secure a quota under the EcbGA; after all, it was brokered by his own organization. Presumably the IMF was not a signatory to the agreement but instead had its interest "recognized" since it was not a "European" organization. And if it had signed, we would have had the usual media frenzy with analysts asking why the U.S. Federal Reserve, the Central Bank of Russia, the Bank of Japan, and others were also not signatories.

In April 2008, Dominique Strauss-Kahn, managing director of the IMF, was able to announce that the institution had agreed to sell 403.3 tonnes of gold, which would be used to create an endowment: "We have made difficult but necessary choices to close the projected income shortfall and put the fund's finances on a sustainable basis, but in the end it will make the fund more focused, efficient, and cost-effective in serving the needs of our members" (see www.imf.org/external/np/sec/pr/2008/pr0874.htm).

On its Web site, the organization states that its "policy on gold is governed by the following principles":

- As an undervalued asset held by the IMF, gold provides fundamental strength to its balance sheet. Any mobilization of IMF gold should avoid weakening its overall financial position.

- The IMF should continue to hold a relatively large amount of gold among its assets, not only for prudential reasons, but also to meet unforeseen contingencies.

- The IMF has a systemic responsibility to avoid causing disruptions to the functioning of the gold market.

◦⟨ Profits from any gold sales should be used whenever feasible to create an investment fund, of which only the income should be used.

For further details, see www.imf.org/external/np/exr/facts/gold.htm.

However, the IMF's plans were derailed by the global financial crisis and the announcements made that culminated in the communique from the London Summit of G-20 nations on April 2, 2009. Among its many clauses was: "We have committed, consistent with the new income model, that additional resources from agreed sales of IMF gold will be used, together with surplus income, to provide $6 billion additional concessional and flexible finance for the poorest countries over the next two to three years. We call on the IMF to come forward with concrete proposals at the Spring Meetings."

On its Web site (at www.imf.org/External/NP/EXR/faq/gold faqs.htm), the IMF makes clear: "On September 18, 2009, the IMF's Executive Board approved gold sales strictly limited to 403.3 metric tons, representing one-eighth of the Fund's total holdings." The IMF further commented:

◦⟨ The Executive Board approved sales strictly limited to the gold the IMF has acquired after the Second Amendment of the Articles of Agreement in April 1978. This amounts to 12,965,649 fine troy ounces or 403.3 metric tons, which represents one-eighth of the Fund's total holdings.

◦⟨ The volume of gold sales approved by the Executive Board is unchanged from the proposed sales in the new income model endorsed by the Executive Board in April 2008, which was also the same volume as recommended by the Crockett Committee in its January 2007 report on the sustainable long-term financing of the IMF.

It is also worth noting that the IMF is something of a special case in its not being allowed to lend its gold, which leads to a dilemma that exists even for the many institutions that can lend gold: the market is too small, and yields are extremely low, to lend a country's entire reserves. Thus, there is a major gap between the nominal size of a central bank's foreign exchange reserves and those that actually earn a yield. Gold is traditionally a buy-and-hold reserve, but many institutions are increasingly being judged on effective management of their holdings; thus the rational decision could be seen to reduce gold reserves and buy an asset that yields a return. It certainly is an argument against holding and/or buying large quantities of gold (in percentage terms), an argument that is increasingly matched by risk aversion in the case of some institutions looking to increase their stock of precious metal.

I know of several instances in which central banks are charged with managing their reserves—the profits are used first to pay for the upkeep of the institution (including salaries) with the excess being remitted to the government—but given the high percentages of gold held and the low yield, they are now unable to meet their running costs. The result has been that the central bank now has to go to the ministry of finance for funds to keep operating. Politically this has been very unpopular and has been behind the sales decision of some of the sellers. Whether this is now outweighed by concerns over counterpart risk, or indeed selling an asset at what might be an under-valued price, is doubtless a key debate.

Who Is Selling and How Much?

The simple answer is that keeping the score under the European central bank Gold Agreement is a lot less easy than some analysts try to make out.

Every Tuesday there is a press release from the European Central Bank at 3 p.m. Frankfurt time, which generally equates to 2 p.m. in London and 9 a.m. in New York. This is the consolidated weekly financial statement of the Eurosystem and shows changes in the overall balance sheet of its members. At the end of each quarter, the data are released one day later, on a Wednesday.

The first problem with this information is that it does not include nations that have signed the gold agreement but are not members of the Eurosystem, Switzerland clearly being the most prominent example. However, it will be interesting to see how the IMF releases its sales figures—those that are sold into the market rather than the press statements detailing transactions with central banks. Indeed, on its Web site the International Monetary Fund noted that it would be transparent as to the method of sales, but it has so far not indicated the mechanism it will use to announce any on-market disposals.

Second, I get very bored with endless news reports telling me that the announcement for the decline in members' gold reserves (expressed in euros) is the quantity of gold that was sold the previous week. It is not—it is merely the difference in the balance sheet: a simple expression of accounting changes. Thus what it actually shows are sales that settled that week. In other words, if a central bank were to sell 10 tonnes of gold and roll it forward for six months, then this transaction would be captured in the ECB's data in six months' time but not next week.

So while it is vaguely useful as a method of keeping score, it is generally irrelevant, particularly so in the early stages of a "quota year." However, once we begin to approach September (each quota year ends on September 26), then the cumulative total has more relevance: if it is considerably less than the year's allocation, then the market can generally take some comfort since it is unlikely that all the gold would either be sold in the final few months or indeed be rolled to that date. Therefore, this is normally seen as a bullish signal.

With the addition of the IMF into the EcbGA, it has become even more difficult. To date the IMF has announced purchases by individual countries, and while it has been open about declaring that it will sell the gold to the market, there has been no word on how this information will be released. As a further twist, I have been told by some commentators that they believe the "off-market" sales (to central banks) are not included under the 400-tonne quota. Personally I find this hard to believe, but there is a lack of clarity, for if this were indeed the case—if there were significant selling from the IMF and European central banks simultaneously—then the market would not take it well.

4

Lenders and Borrowers of Gold

·≋[Who Lends and Borrows Gold?]≋·

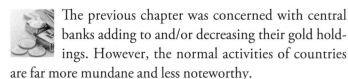The previous chapter was concerned with central banks adding to and/or decreasing their gold holdings. However, the normal activities of countries are far more mundane and less noteworthy.

Generally the managers of a country's wealth seek to maximize the yield of their reserves. In many cases, their role is to handle these reserves efficiently with profits generated to be used for the upkeep of the central bank and any additional to be remitted to the ministry of finance. I must stress that this is by no means true in all countries, but it is a reasonable generalization.

Although the refrain "gold has no yield" is often repeated, it is simply not always true, although it may well be for small holdings. In fact, gold does have an interest rate market comparable to other financial instruments. True, that market is much smaller, but it does exist. The other feature that makes it different is the absence of a central authority directing policy and trying to set rates. Instead, the market is determined purely by supply and demand: the former overwhelmingly from central banks (over 90 percent), while the latter was traditionally seen as gold producers (around 70 percent), physical consignment stocks (around 15 percent), and market shorts making up the balance.

During the 1990s, when producer hedging was at its peak, it was generally estimated that around 4,500 tonnes of gold was lent to the market by central banks before peaking at 4,940 tonnes (according to an estimate from the Virtual Metals Group) toward the end of 2000, roughly one-sixth of total holdings. Some theorists speculated that up to four times as much metal could have been lent as part of a conspiracy to depress the price of gold. One of the outlandish theories was that Germany had lent its entire gold reserves to the Clinton administration in an ultimately unsuccessful attempt to keep the price low (more on this in Chapter 9, "Gold: Myths and Reality").

At this time it was not uncommon for rates to spike as rumors of central bank withdrawals of gold from the market caused some of the less creditworthy bullion banks to become concerned that they would not be able to source sufficient material to service their loan books. In many cases the model adopted by some financial institutions was to lend gold on a long-dated basis (for up to 10 or even 15 years) to mining companies (which were funding their hedge books) while borrowing metal from central banks, or the market, which might be prepared to lend metal only for less than six months. However, the gold interest rate curve was so steep that this practice was deemed a manageable risk.

·◦⟦ The Yield Curve ⟧◦·

The shape of the yield curve has changed little over the years and is generally an upward sloping curve. What has changed, though, is that over the last few years, the entire curve, and hence the yield, has fallen each year until it has ended up as effectively zero. Indeed, apart from a blip higher as banks sought to access cash liquidity via the gold market, the downward trend has been pronounced until it became negative at the front end of the curve at the start of 2010.

Table 4-1 illustrates just that, as demand for borrowed gold has dried up. In each instance that follows, the rate is taken from the first trading day of the year—as a matter of interest, these are where banks would have lent gold but make no allowance for any credit charge (in market parlance they are the LIBOR-GOFO rates).

Table 4-1
Changing Rates of Interest for Gold

	1 MONTH	6 MONTHS	12 MONTHS
1998	1.82%	1.84%	1.94%
1999	0.71%	1.32%	1.63%
2000	0.78%	1.70%	2.12%
2001	0.78%	0.87%	1.37%
2002	0.63%	0.99%	1.43%
2003	0.16%	0.41%	0.71%
2004	0.02%	0.14%	0.34%
2005	0.06%	0.15%	0.18%
2006	0.10%	0.13%	0.14%
2007	0.09%	0.14%	0.17%
2008	0.10%	0.32%	0.32%
2009	0.15%	0.96%	1.07%
2010	−0.13%	−0.01%	0.33%

Since gold interest rates are determined purely by supply and demand—rather than by a central authority—it is clear that one of these dynamics has changed. In this instance it is the borrowing interest (from mining companies) that has dried up—with investors being vocal that they want their equity holdings to reflect exposure to the gold price and not to the hedge book.

As mentioned previously, producers were the vast majority of the borrowers of gold for use in their hedging programs. Considering that the global hedge book was estimated as 3,198 tonnes (Virtual Metals Group and Haliburton Mineral Services) at its peak against 4,940 tonnes of gold being lent, it is reasonably simple to see the influence of this accelerated selling, although the figures are a little overinflated due to the inclusion of options in the overall total.

Because miners were looking to take advantage of the contango in the gold price— defined as the upward sloping price of gold over time—and to protect long-dated cash flows, their interest was to transact at the long end of the curve, in some instances as far out as 15 years. They hedged this exposure to gold interest rates both by locking in long-term rates and by rolling a series of short-term floating ones, three months, for example.

It was clearly much more expensive initially to pay for certainty rather than be exposed to the vagaries of market moves. Consequently, the miners tended to fix only a small proportion of their long-term gold borrowing, preferring to manage their risk via a series of short-term borrows—anything generally from one to six months where there was the greatest liquidity.

◦⟨ Paying Interest in Gold or U.S. Dollars? ⟩◦

Table 4-1 shows the yield in U.S. dollars—expressed in percent—of a gold deposit. A bullet rate of interest is paid in dollars in full at maturity rather than semiannually, and so on. This is a crucial distinction: in fact, in the early 1990s some institutions had not worked out that there was a significant difference for interest rates that paid a return in gold or in U.S. dollars—the longer the tenor, the more dramatic.

The rationale is reasonably simple. If the borrowers and lenders agree that interest should be paid at maturity in U.S. dollars, then the value of the deposit and/or loan is calculated with respect to the spot price. In other words, the interest is the amount of gold multiplied by the spot price (the gold deposit has been "monetized").

If the interest is to be paid in gold and the interest rate is the same, then at maturity the lender will get back the original principal in full plus interest, that is, 1 ounce of gold or $975 (which was equivalent to the original spot price) to be paid at maturity. If lenders know that they will receive 1 ounce of gold in 10 years' time, then they could forward-sell it instead. Because gold is a contango market, they would end up receiving considerably more than $975 for it—in fact, at the time of calculation they would have received $1,420 for that ounce. This difference clearly explains why interest rates that are payable in gold (known as "gold in gold") are different from those in which interest is payable in dollars ("gold in dollars").

In the current environment of low interest rates, it generally makes a difference of a few basis points if any at all, and only then in longer-term rates, but previously it was a significant factor.

It is worth noting though that almost all gold deposits have interest payable in U.S. dollars, which is at the request of the majority of the lenders—the central banks.

The following section should clarify this topic.

·꒛[Calculating Interest on Gold]ꙅ··

The types of trades entered into by the central banks were generally fairly vanilla, and most often they were gold "leases" or "deposits." These two terms do not necessarily denote the same thing, but lazy market jargon uses them interchangeably.

A lease is no different from a money market deposit. In other words, the lender places gold with a bank in return for payment of interest. To clear up a common misconception, if a bank is lent gold, this does not mean that it then has to sell gold and place the dollars gained on deposit. Gold, being a quasi currency, has its own interest rate market, and thus it would be akin to suggesting that should a lender place euros, sterling, yen, or some other currency on deposit, then the borrower would need to enter the foreign exchange market to sell each currency to generate dollars, which are then lent for the interest. This scenario is clearly nonsense; however, the notion was fairly widespread and helped extend the proliferation of conspiracy theories.

An example of a 12-month gold deposit is calculated thus: the lender places 100,000 troy ounces on deposit for 12 months at 20 basis points. At maturity, the central bank has returned to it the 100,000 ounces of gold plus the accrued interest of 202.778 ounces. The calculation is simple:

$$[(100,000 \times 0.20\%)/360] \times 365 = 202.778 \text{ ounces}$$

The day count convention is referred to as "actual over 360."

Most lenders, though, prefer to accumulate interest in U.S. dollars. In that case, a monetary value, basis the then prevailing spot price, is ascribed to gold at the outset of the trade, and the calculation becomes:

$$[(\$975 \times 100,000 \times 0.20\%)/360] \times 365 = \$197,708.33$$

Again principal and interest are returned at maturity. For convenience sake, I have used the same interest rate for a deposit payable in dollars or in gold. In the real market the gold rate would have been slightly lower, as per the above. Where gold is lent for periods longer than one year, the interest is generally paid semiannually, again based on the value of gold at the outset of the trade.

Another way in which gold can be lent is via *lease rate swaps*, also known as "gold interest rate swaps," or just as "gold IRSs." This is dealt with in more depth in the next chapter.

⋅⋅◖ Gold Miners and Hedging ◗⋅⋅

Why Hedge?

It is a myth, I hope, of the gold market that one of the very first hedges done was by an Australian mining company that was impressed that a bank was prepared to buy the gold that the mining company was due to produce in five years at the same price as the current market. Obviously this overlooked the fact that gold is a contango market (so called because the forward curve is upward sloping). Such a trade, if true, would have created an enormous profit for the bank involved.

Indeed, it is this notion of contango that is central to gold hedging. So what is contango?

Contango

For many commodities the natural shape of the price curve is backwardation—that is, the price curve is downward sloping so that the higher price for nearby delivery, over the longer term, reflects convenience yield, the need to have the material readily available (for industrial usage), and the fact that there may be stockpiles available to last only a few days or weeks so that the higher nearby price reflects the relative scarcity of the commodity.

I have read on a number of occasions that since gold prices are upward sloping with time, rather than involving a backwardation, then gold is actually in forwardation. To me *forwardation* is a word bandied about by individuals with little experience in the gold market, and indeed, I have never heard it used in a dealing room. Instead, the term *contango* is universally adopted by traders.

In the examples that follow, I have kept the historic prices (from *Investing in Gold,* which was written in 2008) as it is easier to use them to demonstrate the notion of contango than to use today's prices in their environment of virtually flat curves.

As a concrete example: if a gold mining company were to sell me spot gold (delivery in two business days' time), then I would pay the mining company $975 per ounce on the basis of current market prices. If that same producer wanted to sell me gold but not deliver it for 10 years, then I would pay the producer over $1,400 per ounce.

The calculation itself is simple, as shown in this example:

Spot gold (XAU) = $975

Gold forward rate (GOFO) = 4.50 percent

Days (*t*) = **3,652 (number of days between spot and delivery date)**

The formula is also simple:

$$\text{10-year gold} = \text{XAU} + \{[(\text{XAU} \times \text{GOFO})/360] \times t\}$$

$$= \$975 + \{[(\$975 \times 4.50\%)/360] \times 3652\}$$

$$= \$975 + \$445.088$$

$$= \$1,420.088$$

Incidentally, when gold prices are rolled forward, then it is market convention to use three decimal places for the price. So for deferred delivery, there is the seductive prospect of a premium of $445.088 over the spot price; spot gold is delivered in London and New York two business days after the deal is transacted to allow for delivery of U.S. dollars (in New York) and gold (in London). Surely then it makes sense for companies to hedge at least a portion of their output in future years to protect cash flow and ensure the survival of the mine company.

The notion of contango makes virtually every financial instrument look attractive to the hedger. This is because option pricing models look at the forward price (which includes interest and holding costs, and so on) and determine how far away the strike price is from the notional forward price as one measure of the cost of the option. Using the example above, a mining company may believe that a current gold price of $975 represents a figure at which it is happy to sell metal over the longer term. The option model tells the miner that the cost of this protection for 10 years, buying a put, is $95 per ounce. Is it a price worth paying? Probably yes, when compared to the option struck at the forward price of $1,420, which would cost $255 per ounce.

In many instances, companies have decided that they would rather sell options to gain a premium rather than having to pay for them. Thus a mining company treasurer might have sold a $1,500 two-year gold call for $40, basis a spot price of $975, reasoning that the price is unlikely to rally by such a high percentage over the coming two years. However, there is the potential for problems to occur when there is a loss of control over who determines whether the option is exercised: the owner of the put or call—in my examples, the miner in the first instance but the bank in the second. Thus, while $1,500 might seem an unachievable target over two years, financial grave-yards are littered with the corpses of institutions that rationalized in such a way, the press singling out Long-Term Capital Management as one of the most famous. So if hedging, then it makes sense to hedge only a portion of gold reserves, more perhaps for nearby years than for those further out.

Clearly the argument about hedging is much more nuanced than can be set out in a book of this nature, both because strategies vary and also because they are very dependent on the market's behavior thereafter. If the gold price were to rally strongly from today's levels, then those companies that have recently bought back outstanding hedges would be seen as prescient, whereas those who have been managing their books to ensure the least bad outcome would be seen as dilatory. However, should the converse occur, then the notion of "heroes" and "zeros" changes rapidly.

I think that probably the most eloquent argument in favor of hedging was made at a conference some years ago, when the chairman of a major mining company tried to demystify gold, arguing that a gold producer should act in much the same way as any other company. To illustrate this, he compared running a gold mine to owning a shoe shop. So protect cash flow and run your company as a normal business. Surely sound advice, except that there are many investors who buy equities in gold mining companies because they want exposure to the gold price. They believe that the mines are well managed, and they want to see gold prices rally. Conversely, it seems unlikely that anyone would buy shares in a shoe manufacturer in the expectation of the price of footwear going up.

In effect, there was a disconnect between the way in which some gold producers actually operated and the way in which a number of their shareholders wanted them to perform.

Hedging

During the 1990s, the heyday of forward selling, a rough rule of thumb was that Australian gold miners were the most hedged, followed by North Americans, with South Africans seen as relatively unhedged.

Even within countries practices varied wildly, with some Australian companies apparently hedging at 100 percent of forecast production, and some reputedly even in excess of this as they sought to prosper in the bear market that was gripping the industry. Tactics varied from selling far out of the money (or low delta) short-dated call options of a typical duration of one month or less to locking in the sale price of a proportion of mine production several years out, to 15 years in some instances.

The products themselves could vary from straightforward vanilla sales to complex barrier options that would "knock in" (or "out") if certain parameters were breached on certain dates or a series of dates. These products in turn might be linked to other areas of the producers' hedge book. This interdependence, fortunately not widespread, had great benefits for the treasurers of mining companies if prices remained low, but if gold rallied, they might not only face having to sell metal at submarket prices but also face having to pay a higher interest rate for the gold that they had borrowed. The notion of gold having an interest rate will be alien to some, but it is covered earlier in this chapter.

Lenders and Borrowers of Gold

At its peak, it was estimated by Virtual Metals Group and Haliburton Mineral Services that the global market for gold sold before it had even been mined was 102.8 million ounces (3,198 tonnes). At the end of 2009 these organizations estimated this figure to have fallen to just 7.9 million ounces, or 245 tonnes. Some of these hedges will have rolled off, been allowed to mature, or will have had gold delivered into them, but a large percentage of this gold will have been bought back in the market.

So what changed? The short answer is the gold price, but as to why and whose fault it was that it got so low is a different matter. However, it was certainly an argument that rankled, and particularly during the 1990s when central banks and mining companies each accused the other, sometimes in private and sometimes publicly, of being to blame.

5

Bullion Banks

·≈I Major Trading Centers I≈·

I am no great fan of the phrase "bullion banks," since it seems to be a somewhat ungainly expression, but it is one that simply describes banks involved in the precious metals markets. In the 1990s, Asia/Pacific trading operations were based in Sydney or Melbourne to enable the banks to service the gold mining community, and in particular the prolific hedging activities of the Australian producers, with banks perhaps having other trading centers in Hong Kong or Singapore to supply the physical business (small bars—which generally means those weighing 1 kilo or less). Tokyo was, and still is, obviously the center for the large Japanese trading houses (rather than banks) like Sumitomo, Mitsubishi, and Mitsui. Moving on to Europe, London has always been the main hub, but it was supported by thriving operations in Zurich, Geneva, and Luxembourg. Once the business crosses the Atlantic, there is only one important city, and that is New York. After the market there closes, there is no significant interbank and/or market-making presence until the Asian day once again resumes. With the extension of trading hours, due to online exchanges, this gap is now only about two hours long.

However, the rapid consolidation of the Australian mining industry in the late 1990s, which led, in many instances, to the treasury operations being shifted to Johannesburg or the Americas, meant a sorely diminished customer base. The quieter market conditions that were then prevailing saw rationalization in the industry, with most banks having only one trading operation in each time zone and others sharply curtailing their market-making operations or pulling out of the business completely.

Similarly, it made little sense for an organization to offer market making from London, Geneva, and Zurich, as Credit Suisse used to do when I worked for them in the 1980s, before exiting the business almost completely in 2001 (although its profile has now changed). London became the uncontested preeminent center for European trading. However, in subdued markets, the question then turned to the cost savings from rationalizing operations between Europe and the Americas. Did it make sense to have two complete trading teams based in London and New York when the time difference was only five hours, particularly as COMEX (see Chapter 6 on exchanges) shut its doors at 2:30 p.m. and with it closed the trading day?

For many banks the solution was simple: London should be the center covering both time zones but working longer hours. Obviously this decision became considerably easier when the New York/COMEX floor started closing at 1:30 p.m. local time, thus allowing London traders to leave at 6:30 p.m. their time. However, the growth in the ETFs and the proliferation of online exchanges—particularly the CME Globex—has started to break down this rationale, and the tendency for some form of trading operation in New York has started to become important once more now that trading hours have been extended again.

I have lived and worked in all the major gold-trading centers. Each one has different conventions, customers, and sometimes market makers. However, there are also a great number of similarities. Rather than delve into the minutiae of each particular time zone, I want to look at their similarities. For this I am mainly going to refer to London, not because it is where I am based but because it straddles Asia and the Americas and it is the place where gold "clears" (more on that later in this chapter).

The London Bullion Market Association (LBMA) defines the London market as a "wholesale market, where minimum traded amounts for clients are generally 1,000 ounces of gold and 50,000 ounces of silver. It is an OTC (over-the-counter) market, not an exchange." The LBMA describes itself as "the London-based trade association that represents the wholesale gold and silver bullion market in London. London is the focus of the international Over-the-Counter (OTC) market for gold and silver, with a client base that includes the majority of the central banks that hold gold, plus producers, refiners, fabricators and other traders throughout the world."

Market Makers

The market-making members of the London market recognized by the LBMA are these:

- Bank of Nova Scotia, ScotiaMocatta
- Barclays Bank PLC
- Deutsche Bank AG
- Goldman Sachs International
- HSBC Bank USA NA
- JPMorgan Chase Bank
- Mitsui & Co. Precious Metals, Inc., London Branch
- Société Générale
- UBS AG

So, just nine names form the core of the London market. This number is something of a surprise to many people, who imagine that the gold market is roughly equivalent to the foreign exchange markets and particularly as it is often mentioned along with the dollar, the euro, the yen, and sterling as an essential for central bank reserves. A few years ago, when conditions were quiet, the best guess for daily turnover in the gold market (OTC plus the various exchanges) was roughly equivalent to that of the Polish zloty or Taiwanese dollar. It is now similar to that of the Swiss franc or Canadian dollar. Times have changed, but gold is still a relatively small market.

The Asian and the American time zones have a similar number of interbank market makers, but they do not have an organization such as the LBMA that codifies this. The other important point about this list is that although the LBMA identifies these nine institutions as market makers, a host of other institutions are prepared to make markets for their clients, but are price takers (or market users) of those banks listed previously.

⊸❧ How Does Spot Gold Trade? ❧⊱

When a bank based in Hong Kong trades with one in London, they trade loco London. This trade has nothing to do with where either bank is based but simply where the metal "clears." So similarly when, for example, Mitsui Busan (Hong Kong) trades with Macquarie Bank (Sydney), they too trade loco London UNLESS explicitly stated otherwise, which would be very rare. While I go into more details about clearing later, the simplest definition is where accounts settle—so gold trades "loco London" in the same way that U.S. dollars trade "loco New York" and the yen trades "loco Tokyo." Other locations are possible—if you are a small investor and want to take your bars home with you, then of course you are free to do so. Equally if you work for, say, a sovereign wealth fund, central bank, or asset manager and you want the gold to be in New York, Beijing, Abu Dhabi, Moscow, Zurich, Monte Carlo, Timbuktu, or some other place, then it can be put on a plane (just like banknotes) and delivered. The only hitch is, of course, that you pay for the delivery—depending on the size and location, this might mean anything from a padded envelope to armored trucks, armed guards, chartered cargo planes, motorbike outriders, and a burly team of security-vetted individuals to lift it all. Once there, you of course have to make sure that you have somewhere appropriate to store it.

Back to reality, and the unit of trading is the troy ounce, not the avoirdupois ounce. The latter is the one that we are used to in our daily lives, whereas the former is the unit for weighing precious metal. The troy ounce is roughly 10 percent larger than the avoirdupois ounce (the exact calculation is that 1 troy ounce is equivalent to 1.09714 avoirdupois ounces). Wherever ounces are mentioned in relation to gold in this book, the reference is to troy ounces.

Although the LBMA talks of minimum amounts to clients of 1,000 (troy) ounces of gold, the interbank standard quantity is 5,000 or 10,000 ounces. The underlying unit in this transaction is assumed to be a London Good Delivery bar—in short, a bar weighing between 350 and 430 ounces, which is a minimum of 0.995 gold (995 parts per thousand and generally spoken of as "two nines five"). In reality, the bars generally weigh a few ounces either side of 400, and market shorthand assumes that a bar weighs exactly 400 ounces.

Thus, when one trader makes another a $975/ $976 gold price, then essentially the trader is saying that at $975 he or she would be prepared to buy gold conforming to the specification laid down by the LBMA. However, 5,000 is not evenly divisible by 400, and 12.5 bars of gold is a somewhat tricky concept. Neither is it practical to have a small fleet of heavily armored trucks loaded with gold whizzing through the streets of London. Hence the gold that is generally traded is "unallocated," so that a price of $975 is the bid for an amount of loco London unallocated gold of 99.5 percent purity, and so on. It is worth noting that it is a fine ounce that is actually traded, so what you buy at $975 is the actual gold content rather than the gross weight.

If you own a quantity of allocated gold, then your statement from the custodian (the people running the vault) will detail the bar reference number, its purity, and its fine weight. Assuming you were allowed into the facility, then you could see your gold in its own area (perhaps in a separate cage). However, if you own unallocated gold, then your statement would simply detail the number of ounces in the account. Probably the best analogy is between a checking or current account (unallocated) and a safe deposit box (allocated gold). If you put your dollar bills into a safe deposit box, you know their serial numbers and they are segregated, but if you put your money into a checking account, your money becomes part of the general mass.

Generally most gold accounts held with banks have been for unallocated gold. It is much easier when buying and selling (there is no need for settling weight differences on bars, the costs are less, and there are no concerns over security). That final point might sound strange, but if someone were to rob the bank where you have a checking account, you would be pretty surprised to get a call from the manager telling you that unfortunately the thieves made off with *your* $5,000! However, if there was a break-in and your safe deposit box was rifled, then that is definitely your problem.

Another consideration is that an allocated gold account does not represent credit exposure to the financial institution where you hold your account. In contrast, should the bank where you have an unallocated gold account go bust, then you would have to take your place in line with the other creditors.

Perhaps understandably given the events that engulfed financial centers for much of 2008, the ETFs—which hold allocated gold— became extremely popular as did the practice of switching unallocated gold to allocated gold. It is worth noting that it is relatively easy to switch between accounts for institutional investors, and several have been vocal in their preference for allocated metal, particularly as costs are remarkably similar and in both instances generally considerably cheaper than holding gold via one of the many ETFs.

However, central banks have generally always held gold in allocated form. Commonly, when they trade (spot, forwards, or options), they are trading allocated gold held in their accounts at the Bank of England. Since central banks and members of the LBMA are both allowed to have accounts there, then it is just a simple transfer from one to the other of the various (defined and listed) bars. However, rather than deal 10,000 ounces of gold, for example, the actual quantity needs to be far more exact as it relates to the fine gold content of 25 bars of gold (10,000 divided by 400), so it could be something like 10,006.145 ounces—gold is generally given to three decimal places.

While the normal interbank quantity of gold might be 5,000 or 10,000 ounces, there are a variety of other terms that might be employed by traders and their customers. Rather less common now, outside the gold fixing, is someone trading 5 or 10 bars (4,000 ounces as being 10 bars of 400 ounces each). However, it is not uncommon to trade a tonne; this is assumed to be 32,000 ounces, which is rather different from the precise calculation of a metric tonne as 32,150.70 troy ounces. Equally a trader might be asked for markets in half a tonne, and so forth.

So generally the terminology swings seamlessly between a medieval weight, bars, and metric tonnes (of 1,000 kilograms). However, the market also is equally comfortable using the traditional Indian measurement of lakh, meaning 100,000. Thus being asked for "gold in a lakh" would mean someone requesting a price in 100,000 troy ounces, similarly a half and a quarter of a lakh. While the formal spelling is "lakh," within the market it is generally written as "lac."

So, depending on circumstances, a trader might be asked for a price in ounces, bars, tonnes, or lacs. This may sound unwieldy, but it is quickly picked up and widely adopted. Indeed, for the silver market, it is virtually inconceivable that someone might ask a price in "200,000 ounces"; instead, the request would be for silver in "two lacs."

To clarify a point made previously, I noted that in OTC markets the price is for an ounce of fine gold. Theoretically, if you pay $975 for an ounce of gold, it will physically weigh more than an ounce to account for the impurities. Another way of looking at it is if you were to buy a bar of gold of 401.213 gross weight and a fineness of 0.995, then you would actually be getting 399.207 ounces of gold, and the cost would be this amount multiplied by the spot rate.

·≡| Liquidity |≡·

Given that there are nine spot market makers in London, the greatest concentration globally, then effectively any price request for a quantity over 40,000 ounces of gold becomes significant, the trader offsetting his or her risk by trading with the other eight institutions. Realistically though, in an erratic trading environment, almost any quantity can become unwieldy with prices moving rapidly. However, customers can obtain markets in much greater sizes than this with the interbank traders' exit strategy, enhanced by exchanges and niche market makers who will only quote their client base or show a bid or offer through the brokers.

The method a trader uses to offset risk will vary based on the quantity that has been traded and the market environment. Traditionally, the only tool available to a London-based market maker was to sell to other traders, as it is an OTC market. In contrast, in New York a dealer would probably hedge most of the risk by trading COMEX/NYMEX, and in Asia it would be a combination of one of the local exchanges (Tokyo Commodity Exchange, or TOCOM, is the largest) and direct OTC trades with other market makers.

More recently, the advent of global screen-based exchanges that operate more or less on a 24-hour basis has blurred such precise distinctions, so that traders will all use a combination of OTC, brokers, and exchanges to manage risk—the working of various exchanges is covered in Chapter 6.

Having just outlined these methods, it is difficult to generalize, although I am going to do just that and say that if someone is looking to trade a "significant quantity"—over a tonne, that is, more than 32,000 ounces—then the simplest and/or quickest way to conduct this transaction is going to be in the OTC market.

In some instances, though, institutions need to trade at a "benchmark": a published price that is a matter of record. For the gold market this is invariably the *London gold fixing*.

⊰ The London Gold Fixing ⊱

Given that the first gold fixing took place in 1919, I could use this as an opportunity to embark on a historical tangent on its workings. However, this book is not intended as a record of previous practices except where they affect the current operation of the market. For those who would like to see the timeline, I would recommend viewing the official Web site for the gold fixing—www.goldfixing.com. However, the longest fixing took place on March 23, 1990—caused by a Middle East institution selling a large quantity of gold and buying sterling with it—the price dropping over $20 during the course of this 2-hour, 26-minute marathon, but more typically a fixing is over in 5 to 10 minutes.

That aside, the gold fixing takes place twice daily, at 10:30 a.m. and 3:00 p.m. London time—not GMT as is sometimes reported (GMT is fixed whereas the United Kingdom pushes the clocks forward one hour in summer). The members are the following:

- ⊰ The Bank of Nova Scotia–ScotiaMocatta

- ⊰ Barclays Bank PLC

- ⊰ Deutsche Bank AG

- ⊰ HSBC Bank USA NA

- ⊰ Société Générale

While the names have changed over the years, there have always been five members, and all of these own an equal share in the company that administers the fixing, the London Gold Market Fixing Ltd.

In previous years, representatives met at the London offices of N.M. Rothschild who traditionally chaired the fixing. This might have worked extremely well for many of the last 90 years, but as the financial district of London expanded, it became considerably less convenient with some organizations having to send staff on a

15-minute train ride twice a day to get them from Canary Wharf to Rothschild's headquarters near the Bank of England.

Indeed, there were a number of discussions about moving to either a computer- or phone-based system. Progress had been somewhat slow, but when Rothschild exited the gold market in 2004—citing the declining percentage of total income that commodity trading contributed to its overall profits—the decision was made to end the tradition of the fixing being held in a specific location. Instead, it was conducted over the phone.

Barclays Bank was the newcomer to the fixing at this time, buying the seat vacated by Rothschild. This change also saw the chairing of the fixing rotate on an annual basis. Although the mechanism might have been updated a little, the terminology and methodology remain unchanged.

The fixing now takes place over a dedicated conference line, with each of the five members represented. It starts with the chair suggesting an initial price. This price is then communicated to the five trading rooms, which in turn inform clients via phone, Reuters dealing systems, Bloomberg instant messaging, Yahoo!, and so on. In many instances, these secondary organizations will then inform their clients. At each price any client can buy, sell, or do nothing. All of this information is then collated in the dealing rooms of the five members until it is just a simple amount that needs to be bought, or sold, or is netted off to zero.

Thus each member declares its interest over the phone as buyer, seller, or "no interest." If there are buyers and sellers, or if there are just two of either of those (plus three no interest), then the chair will "call for figures," or announce "trying figures." Each of the five members gives its requested amount in multiples of 5 bars (of a notional 400 ounces each—metal at the fixing is unallocated). If there is a difference of 50 bars or less between the buyers and sellers, then the price is "fixed"—or indeed, between the buyers or sellers and the no interests, with the outstanding balance being divided among the members. Similarly, gold can also be called "fixed" if each of the five banks declares itself a no interest—the conclusion being that the market is in equilibrium at that time.

Traditionally, the selling figures were declared first, perhaps because one of the original purposes of the fixing was to assist the nascent South African mining industry. While this nicety has largely disappeared, the convention is observed in that market shorthand always gives the selling figure first, be it the number of sellers or the bars themselves. Thus "three/one" would mean that there are three sellers and one buyer, whereas "80/20" would mean that 80 bars were offered but only 20 were wanted.

If indeed the balance in the room were 80/20, with each of the five members having declared its interest, the next price to try would be lower, in an attempt to attract buyers and to dissuade sellers. Clearly the situation would be the reverse if the figures were 20/80.

In another piece of relevant history, if a bank wished to change the quantity it had declared or indeed to change its position—from buyer to seller, or the like—then the bank is said to "flag." This term may sound somewhat bizarre, but the term was historically very accurate, although the nature of the act was somewhat odd. When the fixings were held at N.M. Rothschild, each of the five desks in the room was equipped with a small Union Jack, lying on its side. If a member should wish to alter a declaration, then that member would set the flag upright and call "flag." Gold could not, and cannot, be fixed while "flags are up" or "flags are in the room." The same terminology is used in the same way currently, although the Union Jack is now purely figurative.

The attraction of the fixing as a benchmark is clear since it denotes a market that is clearly in balance at that time. Transaction costs are generally very reasonable as well, with both buyers and sellers normally transacting at a premium over the fixing price. This premium might be 5 cents over the price received by sellers and 25 cents charged to buyers. In some instances, it might not be 05/25 but 10/20, in market parlance. The five members transact "in the room" (metaphorical as it might be) in the middle at 15 cents.

ᵉ᷉❘ Trading Gold Interest Rates ❘᷈ᵉ

In Chapter 4, I detailed the borrowers and lenders. In this chapter I want to examine more closely how this market is actually traded.

At its simplest the trading would just be a series of deposits and loans taking place. A central bank lends gold to Barclays Bank, that lends it to a gold producer, which hedges gold that it has yet to produce, and so on. However, trades are not just washed through in exact amounts and tenors (time periods) from one institution to another. No currency market would operate in such a fashion; nor would a series of deposits and/or loans make any sense since the exposure between institutions would build up rapidly and become unwieldy.

Instead, central banks tend to lend gold as a deposit so that full principal risk for the central bank lies on the bullion bank. The banks then trade between themselves via a series of instruments that are designed to mitigate that credit exposure simply to prevent credit lines from being tied up—given the likely high volume of transactions across all traded products. For short-dated trades, the most common mechanism is a "gold swap," also known as a "gold forward." In base metals it would be called a "carry trade," and in money markets a "repo" (sale and repurchase agreement).

Although this is a gold-lending transaction, the mechanism by which it is achieved is via a sale and subsequent repurchase of the metal. The difference in the two prices is calculated using the swap rate, which itself is the theoretical net of U.S. dollar and gold interest rates.

An example, again using historic rates, should make this clearer: Bank A asks Bank B for a six-month gold swap. The price of 2.35/2.45 percent is made. What this means is that at 2.35 percent Bank B would be prepared to lend gold (via a sale and repurchase) and at 2.45 percent it would be prepared to borrow gold (via a purchase and then a sale). Despite the use of "buy" and "sell," these types of transactions have absolutely no impact on the spot price of gold.

Bullion Banks

Assuming that Bank A is a borrower of 100,000 ounces and trades at 2.35 percent:

On Day 1, Bank B sells 100,000 ounces of gold at $975.00 to Bank A.

On Day 180, Bank B buys 100,000 ounces of gold at $986.456 from Bank A.

The forward price is calculated as follows:

$$\$975.00 + \{[(\$975.00 \times 2.35 \text{ percent})/360] \times 180\}$$

$$\$975.00 + \$11.456 = \$986.456$$

$$\text{Gold price} = \{[(\text{gold price} \times \text{gold swap rate})/360] \times \text{day count}\}$$

On the face of it, Bank B has booked a loss on the trade, having sold the gold for $975.00 and bought it back for $986.456, calculated as follows:

$$100,000 \times (\$975.00 - \$986.456) = -\$1,145,600$$

However, from the initial transaction, Bank B has generated $97.5 million (100,000 ounces of gold sold at $975.00 per ounce), which it places on deposit for six months at a rate of 2.50 percent, and this generates interest of $1,218,750. So, Bank B's net profit on the transaction is $73,150 (the interest profit of $1,218,750 less the capital loss of $1,145,600), assuming that it paid zero for the gold originally—which is unlikely, but I just wanted to demonstrate the concept.

Another way of looking at the profit is that it is the net of 2.35 percent (where Bank B borrowed the dollars and lent the gold) and 2.50 percent (where it managed to place the dollars on deposit). This amount of 15 basis points (0.15 percent) is the return for lending gold for six months in this example. Please note that these are historic rates, which I used because, as previously stated, it is easier to illustrate by employing these than to use the current ultra-low-rate environment.

Thus the gold swap rate is the net of U.S. dollar and gold interest rates. It is the gold swap rate market that is the main instrument for short-dated gold trading, and it is this that ultimately drives the lease/deposit market.

Incidentally, the rationale for a central bank lending via a deposit (full principal risk) and a commercial bank lending via swaps (mitigated risk) is not quite as bizarre as it might sound. First, the sheer volume of trades between two market-making institutions is likely to be enormous, so rather than have a jumble of outstandings that might or might not net off, it is a lot easier to mitigate credit risk at the outset. Second, if a central bank were to lend via swaps, then it would generate dollars that would have to be lent to a bank, thus generating the credit risk it tried to avoid in the first place! However, some central banks have used their gold reserves as a form of financing tool—the gold is effectively collateral in a loan.

Interestingly enough, during the recent credit crunch, a two-tier market developed for gold deposits from central banks. Although the highly rated banks might be paying 20 basis points for a 12-month gold deposit from a central bank, I heard of instances in which lenders were being bid 45 basis points (15 basis points above the theoretical offer) by some less creditworthy bullion banks. The attractiveness for the borrower, even paying wildly above the market, was that this gold could subsequently be swapped in the interbank market, thus generating relatively cheap cash for the institution that might be experiencing liquidity constraints. However, such were the concerns over the state of the financial markets that central banks effectively ceased lending gold.

In less turbulent times, for longer-dated transactions the normal style of market transaction is a lease rate swap, gold interest rate swap (or just an IRS, as it is now more commonly referred to). Similarly to the money market instrument—from which it is derived—in market parlance the borrower would "pay fixed and receive floating." In other words, the borrower would borrow fixed-term gold and lend back short-dated. Crucially the gold does not change hands, so it is less credit intensive, but instead, it is the underlying cash flows that are paid and/or received. An example follows: Bank C asks Bank D for a 10-year IRS. A price of 0.65/0.75 percent is quoted. What this means is that at 0.65 percent, Bank D would be prepared to borrow 10-year gold (and lend it back quarterly), and at the other side of the spread, Bank D would be lending the long-dated gold and borrowing it back quarterly.

Assuming that Bank C is a lender of the long-dated gold, then it would trade this at 0.65 percent, lending 10-year gold at that rate and borrowing back over a series of three months. Conversely, Bank D borrows 100,000 at 0.65 percent for 10 years and lends 40 periods of three months each.

Day 1: Bank D agrees that in three months' time it will pay Bank C the following:

$$\{[(\text{Amount of gold} \times \text{fixed interest rate})/360] \times \text{day count}\}$$

$$\{[(100{,}000 \times 0.65 \text{ percent})/360] \times 90\} = 162.50 \text{ ounces of gold}$$

Bank C agrees that in three months' time it will pay Bank D the following:

$$\{[(\text{Amount of gold} \times \text{floating interest rate})/360] \times \text{day count}\}$$

$$\{[(100{,}000 \times 0.16857 \text{ percent})/360] \times 90\} = 42.143 \text{ ounces of gold}$$

Thus net Bank D will pay Bank C 120.357 (that is, 162.50 − 42.143) ounces of gold.

To get the floating interest rate requires a benchmark rate. There is no such number for gold interest rates in the way that there is for currencies. Therefore, convention is that the number is derived from

LIBOR minus GOFO (which is exactly how the market refers to it). LIBOR refers to the benchmark rate for U.S. dollar interest lending rates (published on Reuters page LIBOR) and the benchmark for gold swap/forward rates—GOld FOrward reduced to GOFO, which is also the page where it appears on the Reuters data services.

The above examples are based on the following:

- Three-month U.S. dollar LIBOR of 2.71 percent.

- Three-month GOFO of 2.54143 percent.

- Thus net (LIBOR − GOFO) of 0.16857 percent.

The GOFO benchmark is calculated on a daily basis at 11 a.m. London time. It accepts contributions from nine banks, it discounts the highest and lowest swap rates, and it then derives the final figure from the arithmetic mean of the other seven institutions.

The rationale behind trading the IRS is that it is both a credit-effective way of transacting long-term gold interest rates as well as taking advantage of changes in the shape of the curve—that is, if short-term interest rates start to spike and move above the fixed rate (in the case of an institution that is paying fixed and receiving floating interest amounts).

When central banks lend gold for the long term—realistically in excess of 2 years—they are generally unwilling to take commercial bank credit for periods that might be as long as 10 years. Therefore, to mitigate this risk, they either lend gold on a collateralized basis (the borrowers have to place government bonds with the lender at the same value as the gold, which is reassessed weekly or monthly), or they could enter into an IRS. The problem for the central banks, though, is that a standard IRS does not involve the movement of gold, and the motive for the central banks is to earn a yield on their gold. They do this by lending long-term gold via an IRS, borrowing back the (three-month) gold under the terms of an IRS, but then separately lending gold for the (three-month) short-dated period as well. This may all sound unnecessarily complicated, but in essence it means that they effectively receive a 10-year rate for their gold lending by entering into a series of short-dated trades (40 $\times$ 3 months).

The Gold Option Market

The gold option market functions in much the same way as any currency market. Indeed, gold is often thought of as a currency, although there is admittedly some debate as to whether it is actually a currency or simply a commodity. The safest reply is probably that it has characteristics of both.

The rapid growth in the gold option market (particularly during the 1990s) was driven by the gold mining companies. It occurred for three reasons. First, many of them were consistent sellers of gold call options; second, they were a dominant force for price movements; and third, many of the hedging transactions were large in size and complex.

The rationale for many miners when selling gold call options was twofold. Not only did they recognize that gold was in a long-term bear market but the premium they earned from selling these options was also a welcome addition to their working capital. In most instances the tenor was no more than six months, and some were extremely active in selling options with low delta (small probability of being exercised) for no more than one month, almost seen as money for nothing in the then prevailing bearish environment. However, this complacency meant that there had been rumors that certain small mining companies ended up by selling more call options than their total production for some periods. Indeed, this was rumored to be behind some of the difficulties faced by certain mining companies when gold spiked following the central bank gold agreement in September 1999: the price of the options suddenly became too expensive to buy back, and they had insufficient gold production to meet the calls that were being exercised.

The producers were as dominant in call selling as they were in put buying—obviously their natural hedge—so that a major skew arose in put volatility: it was much more expensive than that for calls.

To generalize, not particularly unfairly, during the hedging hey-day of the market, the independent Australian producers were the most active. They were also extremely innovative—or at least very interested in entering into innovative trades—and prepared to use linkages across markets and structures that defaulted into different basis risk. Indeed, when I was part of a presentation team to a mining company in the late 1990s, they were not interested in any of the more vanilla structures but wanted the most leveraged option possible; they were sellers and wanted to realize the greatest amount of premium.

The trouble was that there was little in the way of effectively measuring the risk for many of these institutions, and in certain instances they did not, or could not, stress-test their books to see what would happen under various scenarios. Again the result was considerable angst when the gold market started to rally, first during late 1999 and then in subsequent years. I remember helping an Australian mine evaluate its hedges, which had a high degree of linkage between spot gold and gold interest rates. For example, should gold rise, this would then ratchet up the interest rate the company needed to pay for borrowing gold. Thus a sudden rapid spike in prices would have led to an untenable and unmanageable situation for the miner. Hence the firm subsequently restructured its hedge-book to help protect against this eventuality.

This company was not alone in this type of hedging. In most instances these positions were unwound, and ultimately a lot of the small independent producers were taken over by large offshore companies.

The demands of the gold producers at this time saw a period of great innovation in the type of option structures that could be entered into. First of all, there were just vanilla puts and calls; these were soon joined by barrier options, window and anniversary barriers, digitals, quantos, and so on. Most of these were designed to meet the payoff requirements of the mining industry, although many of the ideas were imported from the foreign exchange and fixed income markets.

Obviously matters are very different now. The producers are far less inclined to hedge; indeed, that business has almost entirely ground to a halt. Pronouncements by miners on this topic are far more likely to be that they have foresworn this activity—and the only exception really is when banks demand hedging as a precondition of lending money to a new project—in effect, ensuring prudent cash-flow protection.

·◦[Hedge Funds]◦·

Hedge funds have been active in the gold market for many years. However, the rapidly growing amount of assets under management (AUM)—now estimated to be $1.875 trillion—has seen their influence increase rapidly even as that of the producers has declined. Indeed, for the 1990s it was undoubtedly the gold mining companies and the central banks (to fund the hedges) that were the most actively targeted customers for bullion banks; now it is hedge funds. However, with the various concerns over the state of the global financial system and most tellingly whether sovereign debt is indeed as riskless as was thought, there is a great deal of growing interest in gold from wealth managers, ranging from sovereign wealth funds to pension and mutual funds. It is this type of investor that is key to gold's longer-term future—those organizations looking for an investment that does not represent a risk to anyone else. I do not believe that we are going to see asset managers suddenly putting 50 percent of their funds into gold, but they might well believe that even 5 percent or less represents sensible "insurance" against the rest of the financial system. In what is a small market, this would have a dramatic impact.

Initially, hedge fund activity in gold was limited to specialist commodity funds with considerable input from macro hedge funds with long-standing commodity interest. For those who are unaware of what "macro hedge funds" actually are: basically they do not specialize in any one particular market or sector; instead, their expertise and product suite is wide ranging. However, the rapid growth in AUM has meant that funds are increasingly looking to new markets in which to invest. The fact that this rapid increase in the power of this particular sector has coincided with the decline in the U.S. dollar has been a considerable help to the gold price.

While there have always been people who are interested in gold, be they "gold bugs" or just enthusiasts for their own purposes, for many in the 1990s, it had become an obsolete form of investment. Why bother to invest in gold as an inflation hedge when you could buy Treasury Inflation-Protected Securities (TIPS) instead? People fleeing oppression and war did not need gold; all they needed was a halfway decent banking system, or Internet connection, to transfer money overseas. Central banks had never enjoyed such high levels of esteem or belief in their powers to rein in inflation. Gold generally has no yield for the small, private investor, so what was the point of investing in it? Indeed, being in the gold market during the dot-com boom looked to be a lesson in futility.

This trend was the ultimate expression of how gold had been marginalized. Entrepreneurs were creating enormous wealth with little more than a business plan. What did people need with a stale and stagnant gold market? Clearly there were much better places for investment; indeed, for many the ideal trade would have been to short gold (the ultimate expression of the "old economy") while buying technology stocks.

The change in the fortunes of many Internet stocks and the U.S. dollar has been a wake-up call for the attractions of gold—hence the belief of hedge funds in this market that has seen them become a significant influence. Once more they are looking at products similar to those that they use in other markets to participate in the rise of gold. However, no one should be under any illusions; this interest is rarely long term. It is not a replacement for buying from central banks, wealth managers, and the like; instead, it is taking advantage of the current market outlook. Once this view changes, there will be no emotional attachment to gold. Instead, there is the possibility of finding a very crowded exit. Most hedge funds are ambivalent as to whether they are trading copper, cocoa, corn, coffee, credit default swaps, Canadian dollars, Chinese yuan, or Colombian pesos—it is the story behind it, such as a fundamental view or a technical/chart picture, that piques their interest. For the avoidance of doubt, many hedge funds are solely interested in momentum. They will buy a rising market and sell a falling one. Their views are not colored by emotion but solely by performance.

In many situations, hedge funds will go with the consensus view (or perhaps create it). They certainly have little interest in being continual sellers of call options in rising or falling markets. Instead, they will tend to buy call options if they believe the market is rising (or sell puts) and the converse if they believe the market is falling. Hence, in rising markets, there is a premium for call volatility over that for puts and the opposite when prices are falling.

For the interbank option market there are probably just six "first-division" players with another four in the second tier. The standard interbank quote is 50,000 to 100,000 ounces (half a lac or a lac) out to one year, but volumes tend to fall away after that. Large customers can fairly easily obtain prices in considerably larger volume. The standard convention within the gold market has been to ask for a gold call or put, perhaps even as "an Aussie gold call" if there is interest to trade gold against a currency other than the dollar. Indeed, I think it is vital to look at gold's performance in other currencies, particularly the euro, to divorce the performance of gold from the noise created by currency markets. However, the market is increasingly adopting language garnered from the foreign exchange market such that it is commonly referred to as a "gold call U.S. dollar put" or perhaps a "gold put Aussie dollar call," and so on.

Generally though, market makers will tend to make markets in gold against U.S. dollars, Australian dollars, euros, and the South African rand—Aussie dollars and the rand being holdovers from the days of hedging from the mining industry. Realistically though, the U.S. dollar gold option market accounts for some 80 percent of all business, the Australian dollar a further 10 percent, and the other currencies are very much also-rans. However, the recent ructions in the fortunes of the Eurozone have seen the gold price rally sharply against that currency and with it a dramatic increase in the amount of business transacted in gold against the euro.

While, theoretically, it is no harder to make prices against the Canadian dollar, Swiss franc, or Japanese yen, the vol (market shorthand for volatility) bid-offer spread will tend to be considerably wider and only really entered into for significant business.

In the end, all business, be it spot, forward, or options, needs to be "cleared."

·⊰ Clearing ⊱·

As mentioned previously, London is the clearing center for gold in exactly the same way that the U.S. dollar clears through New York and the yen through Tokyo. The London Bullion Market Association (LBMA) defines this process as follows: "The London bullion market relies on a daily clearing system of paper transfers. Members offering clearing services utilize the unallocated gold and silver accounts they maintain between each other for the settlement of mutual trades as well as third-party transfers. These transfers are conducted on behalf of clients and other members of the London bullion market in settlement of their own loco London bullion activities. This system avoids the security risks and costs that would be involved in the physical movement of bullion."

Indeed, the notion of a succession of trucks laden with gold bullion making their way through the streets of the City of London, and its environs, would create a logistical and security nightmare, as well as significantly increase transaction costs. Anecdotally, a couple of short examples illustrate this scenario. One story is that of a European central bank that had entered into a gold-lending program, and all of the agreements had the same maturity date. Because the gold had to be returned to the Bank of England, a line of armored trucks was parked outside that institution's vaults while the metal was unloaded. Suffice it to say, that particular trading strategy was never used again. Another story involves an armored truck managing to hit the security doors of a clearer's vaults, rendering the depository out of action for several days. Clearly accidents do happen, and it is sensible to avoid them whenever possible.

There are six companies that offer a clearing service, and they are joint owners of a company called London Precious Metals Clearing Limited (LPMCL):

- Barclays Bank PLC

- The Bank of Nova Scotia, ScotiaMocatta

- Deutsche Bank AG, London Branch

- HSBC Bank USA National Association, London Branch

- JPMorgan Chase Bank

- UBS AG

Traditionally, banks tended to provide clearing services free of charge because vaults were unlikely to ever be full of metal, which meant that the clearers could lend out balances held in their vaults (unallocated only), which in turn mitigated the cost. This service worked very well when there was a vibrant lending and borrowing market. However, when turnover sharply decreased (the virtual demise of the gold hedging market is covered in Chapter 4), vaults did start to fill, and there was little call to borrow gold.

It was at this time that a once-free service began to be charged for; indeed, one-month interest rates were trading at −10 basis points (minus 0.1 percent) at one stage, and thus storage of gold just became a charge with no possibility of lending the metal to cover costs.

While the metal can theoretically be transferred throughout the trading day, in practice it tends to happen just prior to 4 p.m., London time, when transfers should stop, except by mutual consent.

There is one extremely important institution that also clears metal but has not been mentioned above and is not a part owner of LPMCL: it is the Bank of England. The vaults of the bank lie outside the clearing system because all movements there are allocated—hence the above-described truck lineup. In other words, specific bars are transferred from one account to another. The largest group of institutions that choose to maintain their accounts at the Bank of England are the central banks; by contrast, I can think of only six countries that maintain unallocated accounts at a clearer (and most of these have accounts at the Bank of England as well).

·≡[Turnover]≡·

In the London market—where gold of course clears for OTC transactions—the relevant data are compiled by the LBMA, which collates, on a monthly basis, information provided to it from the six members offering clearing services (LPMCL). Three measures are taken separately for each metal:

> **Volume:** The amount of metal transferred on average each day measured in millions of troy ounces. (See Figure 5-1.)

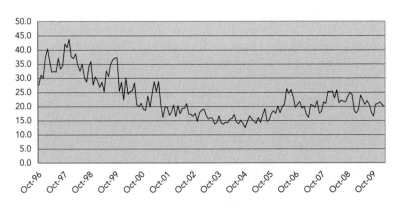

Figure 5-1

Ounces of Gold Transferred Daily in London (in Millions)

Source: London Bullion Market Association (LBMA)

Bullion Banks

Value: The value measured in U.S. dollars, using the monthly average London afternoon fixing price for gold. (See Figure 5-2.)

Number of Transfers: The average number recorded each day. (See Figure 5-3.)

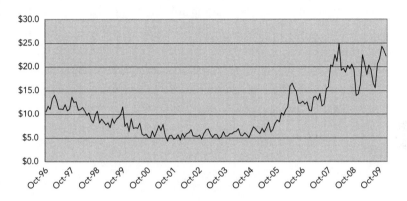

Figure 5-2

Value of the Gold Transferred Daily in London (in USD Billions)

Source: London Bullion Market Association (LBMA)

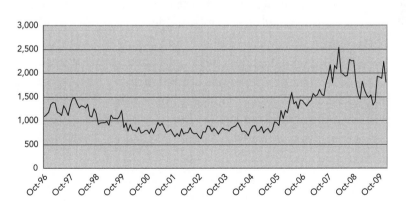

Figure 5-3

The Average Number of Transfers of Metal Each Day in London

Source: London Bullion Market Association (LBMA)

It is worth remembering that gold is a small market with OTC/ loco London settlement of traditionally less than $15 billion on a daily basis, although it is currently running at roughly $22.2 billion basis according to the LBMA statistics for January 2010.

However, turnover is likely to be a multiple of settled ounces, particularly adding in the various exchanges. It is difficult to put any sort of exact number on it, but taking an educated guess, and as mentioned earlier, it would seem sensible to equate the gold market with being somewhere between the USD/CAD (U.S. dollar versus Canadian dollar) and USD/CHF (U.S. dollar versus Swiss franc) markets. Incidentally, the global foreign exchange market turns over some $3 trillion on a daily basis.

·⊰ Market Conventions ⊱·

Spot Market Making

The general interbank "clip" is for 5,000 to 10,000 ounces of gold. However, it is standard for all price requests to include the quantity. Thus market shorthand is "gold in 10k" or similarly expressed. Market makers do not ask each other in prices for smaller than 5,000 ounces as it is assumed, rightly, that they are risk takers with a flow of transactions through their books and lesser quantities would be unprofessional.

Aside from the nine London market makers listed earlier in this chapter, a number of institutions are prepared to provide prices to their customer base but not to other market makers. These market users will either try to "broker" transactions to the market makers making a small turn on the trade, or they will hedge their risk through the myriad exchanges (which are covered in Chapter 6).

Bullion Banks

Options Market Making

The standard quantity is 50,000 to 100,000 ounces, but it will depend on tenor, volatility, delta, and currency pairing. In regard to customers, the same comments apply here as above.

Forwards Market Making

Once again, the standard traded quantity is 50,000 to 100,000 ounces, but it will very much depend on the tenor, with customers often able to gather quotes in increased size at more favorable terms.

6

Gold Exchanges

Throughout this book, it has been my intention to approach matters chronologically, and thus I am starting with the various exchanges in Asia before proceeding to the United States via the newest player in Dubai, as well as the ever-present online futures markets. My apologies if I have omitted a particular institution, but I have concentrated on those markets where professionals tend to focus their attention—and not yet on the at least three new contracts that various exchanges are trying to launch to capture the enormous interest in gold.

⊰ TOCOM (Japan) ⊱

TOCOM is the universally adopted acronym for the Tokyo Commodity Exchange. It defines itself (www.tocom.or.jp) as follows: "TOCOM is a nonprofit membership organization as defined under the Commodity Exchange Act (1950), which regulates all commodities futures and options trading in Japan."

The specifications of the contract that is traded there, again from the exchange's Web site, are listed as follows:

Date of Listing: March 23, 1982

Type of Trade: Physical delivery futures transaction

Standard: Fine gold of minimum 99.99 percent purity

Trading Method: Computerized continuous trading

Contract Months: All even months within a year (On the day when a new contract month is generated, there will be six even months starting from the next even month after the month which the said day belongs to.)

Last Trading Day: The third business day prior to the delivery day

Delivery Day: The last day of each even month except December (the 24th for December). If the day is a holiday or a half-day holiday, the delivery day is advanced.

Delivery Points: Specified warehouses

Trading Hours: Day session 9:00 a.m. to 3:30 p.m. (JST); night session 5:00 p.m. to 11:00 p.m. (JST)

Contract Unit: 1 kilogram per contract

Delivery Unit: 1 kilogram per contract

Price Quotation: Japanese yen per gram

Minimum Price Fluctuation: One Japanese yen per gram

Daily Price Fluctuation Limit: Daily price fluctuation limits are determined based on the largest market price movement within a certain time period and set at a level where the probability that they will be reached is very low.

In addition to the underlying contract, you need to know how to actually trade on the exchange. Here too the TOCOM Web site sets out its order and/or execution system.

Gold Exchanges

The following describes the methods for participating in TOCOM's markets from overseas:

1. **As a Member:** To access TOCOM's markets directly, you are required to obtain Market Membership and install a TOCOM trading terminal in Japan (direct access).

2. Members without a trading terminal can trade on TOCOM's markets through TOCOM Broker Members (indirect access—through Futures Commission Merchants or FCMs).

3. In either case, eligibility for membership is limited to foreign FCMs and persons or firms engaged in the purchase or sale, brokerage, production, processing, or use of commodities listed on the Exchange, who meet certain financial and other qualifications. In addition, certain financial obligations are required to be a member.

4. **As an Associate Member:** Overseas traders who deal with commodities listed on TOCOM's markets and belong to certain organizations specified by TOCOM are eligible for Associate Membership. Associate Membership is like a special favored customer status—that is, Associate Members must place orders through Broker Members and have no right of voting at general meetings, but the same margin rates applied to Members are applied to Associate Members.

5. **As a customer:** You can place an order as a customer with a Broker Member. Also, your order can be accepted by a Foreign FCM who places the order through a Broker Member to TOCOM.

All of the foregoing is useful information, but the majority of us simply need to know how it relates to the loco London gold price and if there is an effective arbitrage.

Because TOCOM gold contracts are available only for alternate even-numbered months, the eleventh or twelfth month forward is the active contract, depending on the actual date (that is, in January it is December that is the most traded, and in July it is June, and so on). So to determine whether there is an effective arbitrage, we need to convert yen per gram for delivery in 11 months, for example, to U.S. dollars per troy ounce for delivery in two days. Added to which there is a difference in the underlying bar size (kilo rather than 400 ounce) and purity (9999 rather than 995). That is to say that TOCOM trades "four nines" purity gold (99.99% pure) as against London's "two nines five" (99.5% pure). Finally, there is the difference in delivery location—Tokyo against London.

The final conundrum is that foreign traders have occasionally been uncertain as to their rights to deliver onto the exchange. The rules seem to be somewhat clearer for Japanese houses based there, in which case the arbitrage can "blow out" rather further than the pure mathematics would suggest. Consequently, most foreign institutions choose not to deliver metal into TOCOM.

The rough calculation itself is as follows:

L = **Loco London spot price in dollars per ounce**

T = **TOCOM price expressed in Japanese yen per gram**

C = **32.148 = conversion factor for 9999 purity gold in grams to ounces**

F = **Forward foreign exchange rate to convert the contract to U.S. dollars**

S = **Swap rate to convert a forward gold price to a spot equivalent**

$$L = [G \times (1{,}000/32.148)]/[F \times (1 + S)]$$

Clearly this is much less complicated once the appropriate spread-sheet has been completed.

⮞ Chinese Gold and Silver Exchange Society (Hong Kong) ⮜

Arguably the world's oldest exchange for trading precious metals, it began in 1910 as the "Gold and Silver Exchange Company" before changing its name in 1918 to "The Chinese Gold and Silver Exchange Society" (CGSE)—the name it still goes by.

Despite its age, this exchange has lost a considerable amount of its importance from its heyday, which was probably in the 1970s and early 1980s, before it found its position eroded by TOCOM. Once again the units, purity, bar size, location, and so on, all vary from the recognizable spot price for gold.

The exchange currently trades in two methods: one is the "open outcry" method in its trading hall, and the other is the "electronic trading" method via its electronic trading platform, which launched in March 2008.

Open Outcry Market

The exchange itself varies from TOCOM in that it is an open outcry market and it is conducted in Cantonese, the local language. Unusually, for any exchange, it has two gold products that are traded. The first is the traditional taels with a kilogram price having been added in 2002. The Web site of the Chinese Gold and Silver Exchange Society (www.cgse.com.hk) defines the contracts as follows:

Open Outcry Market in Taels

>   **Fineness:** 99
>
>   **Trading Lot:** 100 taels
>
>   **Price Indication:** Hong Kong dollar per tael

Minimum Price Fluctuation: 0.50 Hong Kong dollar per tael

Premium Calculation: Hong Kong dollar per 100 taels

Premium Fixing: Monday to Friday 11:00 a.m.

Settlement Price: Monday to Friday 11:30 a.m. to 4:30 p.m.

Open Outcry Market in Grams

Fineness: 9999

Trading Lot: 5 kilograms

Price Indication: Hong Kong dollar per gram

Minimum Price Fluctuation: 0.10 Hong Kong dollar per gram

Premium Calculation: Hong Kong dollar per 5 kilograms

Premium Fixing: Monday to Friday 11:15 a.m.

Settlement Price: Monday to Friday 11:30 a.m. to 4:30 p.m.

I doubt whether many people who have not spent time in Asia are particularly conversant with the term *tael*, but it is an ancient Chinese unit of weight, a little larger than a troy ounce. To convert a tael to a troy ounce, the tael amount needs to be divided by 0.831.

Obviously there are again the same issues of purity, bar, location, and so on. However, a very rough guide to convert the price on this Hong Kong (HK) exchange to a loco London spot equivalent is as follows:

L = **Loco London spot price in dollars per ounce**

HK = **CGSE price expressed in HK dollars per tael**

C = **1.1913 = conversion factor for 99 purity gold in taels to ounces**

F = Foreign exchange rate to convert the contract to U.S. dollars (called the TT rate)

$$L = (HK/1.1913)/F$$

Incidentally, although I spent six years working in Hong Kong's gold markets, I never calculated a price in taels per Hong Kong dollar. I had a physical trader who used the market to arbitrage his positions in the local and/or international markets, as well as helping me manage my loco London positions via the exchange on occasions where there was sufficient liquidity. Instead, whether I was trading with another bank in Hong Kong or with a bank in Tokyo, Sydney, Singapore, Beijing, and so on, we were trading loco London gold between us: in other words, U.S. dollars per troy ounce for settlement in London two days later.

I have not included the calculation for the kilogram contract, as I understand that the turnover has been extremely small.

Electronic Trading Platform

There are two types of contract, which are the 100-ounce Loco London Contract and the 10-ounce Loco London Contract traded via the electronic system, the details of which are as follows:

Fineness: Pure gold

Trading Lot: 100 ounces and 10 ounces

Price Indication: U.S. dollar per ounce

Minimum Price Fluctuation: U.S. dollar 0.01 per ounce

Settlement Price: Average price at a specific time frame

Premium Calculation: Determined by the Executive and Supervisory Committee, based on a specific time frame

Premium Fixing: With reference from the LBMA

Delivery: 400-ounce gold bar of 995 fineness, produced by refinements of the LBMA good delivery list

Trading Hours: (Hong Kong Time) 8:00 a.m. to 3:30 p.m. (next day), Monday through Friday

Shanghai Futures Exchange (China)

On its Web site (www.shfe.com.cn/Ehome/index.jsp), the exchange describes itself as "a self-regulated nonprofit organization, providing the place, facilities, and services for the centralized trading of futures contracts. At present, there are six contracts including copper, aluminum, natural rubber, fuel oil, zinc, and gold futures."

The contract itself is defined on the Shanghai Futures Exchange Web site as follows:

Underlined Product: Gold

Trading Unit: 1 kilogram per lot

Quotation Unit: yuan (RMB) per gram

Tick Size: 0.01 yuan per gram

Daily Price Limit: Within range of 5 percent above or below the settlement price of the previous trading day

Contract Months: January to December

Trading Hours: 9:00 a.m. to 11:30 a.m.; 1:30 p.m. to 3:00 p.m.

Last Trading Day: The fifteenth day of the spot month (postponed if legal holidays)

Delivery Duration: The sixteenth to twentieth day of the spot month (postponed if legal holidays)

Deliverable Grades Domestic Product: Gold with fineness not less than 99.95 percent

Overseas Product: Gold that is regarded by the LBMA as good delivery

Delivery Sites: Warehouses designated by the exchange

Minimum Transaction Margin: 7 percent of contract value

Transaction Fee: Equal to or below 0.02 percent of transaction value (risk reserve included)

Delivery Method: Physical delivery

Symbol: AU

Listed Bourse: SHFE

The six-month forward month is generally the active contract. The approximate calculation to compare this to the loco London spot gold price is as follows:

L = **Loco London spot price in dollars per ounce**

G = **SHFE price expressed in Chinese yuan per gram**

C = **32.1355 conversion factor for 9995 purity gold in grams to ounces**

F = **Forward foreign exchange rate to convert the contract to U.S. dollars**

S = **Swap rate to convert a forward gold price to a spot equivalent**

$$L = [G \times (1{,}000/32.135)]/[F \times (1 + S)]$$

⇥ Dubai Gold and Commodities Exchange (Dubai) ⇤

The Dubai Gold and Commodities Exchange (DGCX) is the newcomer to the stable of gold exchanges and is making a strong push to grow its business. The DGCX commenced trading in November

1995 and offers "fully automated, state-of-the-art, electronic trading accessible from anywhere in the world."

On its Web site (www.dgcx.ae), the DGCX defines its contract as follows:

Contract Size: 32 troy ounces (1 kilogram)

Quality Specification: 0.995 purity, as per Dubai good delivery standard

Trading Months: February, April, June, August, October, and December

Last Trading Day: Business day immediately preceding the sixth delivery day

New Contract Listing: On the last delivery day

Price Quote: U.S. dollar per troy ounce

Minimum Tick Size: U.S. dollar 0.10

Price Movement Limit: Thirty U.S. dollars (for more details see the Web site)

Maximum Open Position Limit: As determined and specified by the exchange

Maximum Order Size: 200 contracts

Trading Days: Opening: Monday through Friday

Trading Hours: Monday through Friday, 8:30 a.m. to 11:30 p.m. (GMT + 4)

For delivery:

Delivery Unit: 1 kilogram (31.99 troy ounces)

Deliverable Weight: 1 kilogram cast in one bar

Deliverable Quality: 0.995 fineness

Approved CMI/Assayers: Names as listed on the DGCX Web site

Approved Refiners: Names as listed on the DGCX Web site

Approved Vaults: Names as listed on the DGCX Web site

Delivery Period: First through sixth delivery day of the delivery month

First Notice Day: Business day immediately preceding first delivery day

Last Notice Day: Business day immediately preceding sixth delivery day

Delivery Process: Compulsory delivery as allocated by the exchange on a random basis

Vault Charges: Rates applicable as published on the DGCX Web site

Delivery Instrument: Dubai Gold Receipt (DGR) (that is, a Standard DGR along with validated refiner's certificate or CMI-Certified DGR only)

The calculation to convert this to a loco London spot gold price is considerably easier than for the three previous exchanges since there is no currency, purity, or weight factor to take into account—the quoted unit is U.S. dollars per troy ounce—so it is done in the same way as for the New York Mercantile Exchange (NYMEX):

$$[(\text{Loco London spot gold price} \times \text{gold forward rate})/360] \\ \times \text{ day count to delivery day}$$

This would then represent the exchange of futures for physicals (EFP), which would need to be subtracted from the exchange price to obtain an equivalent loco London spot equivalent.

⊰ New York Mercantile Exchange (United States) ⊱

There is, as yet, no widely followed gold exchange in Europe. Instead, there is a leap in the exchanges that goes from Asia (where TOCOM remains the most important) to New York—trading in Europe is predominantly OTC.

On its Web site (www.nymex.com), the New York Mercantile Exchange, Inc., defines itself as "the world's largest physical commodity futures exchange and the preeminent trading forum for energy and precious metals. The gold contract is available for trading via open outcry on the COMEX Division of the Exchange as well as electronically on CME Globex":

> The Exchange has stood for market integrity and price transparency for more than 135 years. Transactions executed on the Exchange avoid the risk of counterparty default because the NYMEX clearinghouse acts as the counterparty to every trade. Trading is conducted in energy, metals, softs, and environmental commodity futures and options via the CME Globex® electronic trading system, open outcry, and NYMEX ClearPort®.

This exchange has yet another set of contract specifications. NYMEX defines these as follows:

> **Trading Unit:** 100 troy ounces
>
> **Price Quotation:** U.S. dollars and cents per troy ounce
>
> **Trading Hours:** Open outcry trading is conducted from 8:20 a.m. until 1:30 p.m. (All times are Eastern Standard Times.) Electronic trading is conducted from 6:00 p.m. until 5:15 p.m. via the CME Globex trading platform, Sunday through Friday. There is a 45-minute break each day between 5:15 p.m. (current trade date) and 6:00 p.m. (next trade

date). Off-exchange transactions can be submitted solely for clearing to the NYMEX ClearPort clearing Web site.

Trading Months: Trading is conducted for delivery during the current calendar month; the next two calendar months; any February, April, August, and October falling within a 23-month period; and any June and December falling within a 60-month period beginning with the current month.

Minimum Price Fluctuation: 0.10 (10 cents) per troy ounce ($10 per contract).

Last Trading Day: Trading terminates at the close of business on the third to last business day of the maturing delivery month.

Delivery: Gold delivered against the futures contract must bear a serial number and identifying stamp of a refiner approved and listed by the exchange. Delivery must be made from a depository licensed by the exchange.

Rules and Provisions: Complete delivery rules and provisions are detailed in Chapter 113 of the Exchange Rulebook.

Delivery Period: The first delivery day is the first business day of the delivery month; the last delivery day is the last business day of the delivery month.

Exchange of Futures for Physicals (EFP): The buyer or seller may exchange a futures position for a physical position of equal quantity. EFPs may be used to either initiate or liquidate a futures position.

Grade and Quality Specifications: In fulfillment of each contract, the seller must deliver 100 troy ounces (65 percent) of refined gold, assaying not less than 995 fineness, cast either in one bar or in three one-kilogram bars, and bearing a serial number and identifying stamp of a refiner approved and listed by the exchange. A list of approved refiners and assayers is available from the exchange upon request.

Position Accountability Levels and Limits: Any one month/all months: 6,000 net futures equivalent, but not to exceed 3,000 in the spot month.

Margin Requirements: Margins are required for open futures positions.

Trading Symbol: GC

Once again we are looking at U.S. dollars per troy ounce and for gold of 995 fine, which makes the rough guide calculations somewhat easier.

For traders looking to arbitrage the COMEX gold contract against London gold, the calculation is very simple. Essentially it is assumed that the two locations are absolutely fungible. Thus at its simplest, it is just the outright forward gold contango for each month that is the underlying calculation (below)—given the ease of converting 400-ounce bars to 100-ounce bars, particularly as they happen to be the same purity, and the large number of flights between London and New York. However, and as with all the exchanges listed above, the simple assumptions inherent in the calculation will vary on the basis of local conditions. To take a dramatic example, if all flights between the United Kingdom and the United States were grounded, then clearly the EFP would be impacted, as the arbitrage would no longer be operational.

As above, EFP stands for "exchange of futures for physical" and simply means the differential between 100 ounce bars trading for a future date in New York and 400 ounce bars trading spot and clearing in London. Thus, if there are any problems shipping metal from one location to the other, the cost basis will clearly change.

In general though, gold trades actively on COMEX for the February, April, June, August, and December contracts; the October contract is normally skipped in terms of the "active" month (the front month contract with the most open interest).

Thus, if the date today were September 1, then the active contract would be December. The theoretical EFP should be the following:

$$[(\text{Loco London spot gold price} \times \text{gold forward rate}) / 360] \times \\ \text{day count to December 15}$$

$$[(\$975 \times 2.50\%)/360] \times 91$$

$$= 6.16 \text{ as a midrate}$$

Therefore, a market maker might well quote $6.05/6.25. Just to reiterate, this is the theoretical rate and not where it necessarily might be trading; instead, it gives a rough guide.

Online Exchanges

TOCOM is, by its charter, an online exchange, whereas NYMEX started life as an open outcry exchange and has supplemented this business with its online activities. It is the extended trading hours provided by the latter that has seen its relevance and volumes increase even further.

Whereas Europe has always been primarily an OTC market, the reach of the CME Globex trading platform has meant that Asian and European market makers have added this to their armory of risk management tools.

A Health Warning!

In each instance, these calculations can only be rules of thumb and are, at best, no more than approximations. Outside the straight mathematical value suggested by these formulas, there may be local conditions that see the EFP (the differential between the cash and futures market) trade very differently in practice to where it should theoretically trade and for far longer than might be supposed: the old trading maxim about markets remaining irrational for far longer than an investor remaining solvent.

So while matters should ultimately correct themselves, it may not be before a trader has lost either his or her job or a considerable amount of money—or both. So while there may look to be arbitrage opportunities, this can be deceptive.

It is also worth noting that in each case I have provided rough calculations to convert somewhat esoteric sounding contracts (perhaps none more so than Hong Kong dollars per tael) back to a loco London format. However, for many individuals this is not even relevant as their entire exposure, or interest, to gold is in yuan or yen per gram, and so on, and thus the arbitrage is immaterial.

7

Exchange-Traded Funds

ᵒ∫ What Is an Exchange-Traded Fund (ETF)? ∫ᵒ

 The ETF is a relatively new feature of the precious metals markets. A definition, which is provided on www.ishares.com, is that "an Exchange-Traded Fund (ETF) is an investment vehicle which is constructed as an open-ended collective investment scheme and trades like an individual security on a stock exchange. In the eyes of the retail investor, they are perhaps best thought of as a mutual fund/stock hybrid."

More specifically gold ETFs are designed to track the price of gold, less the storage and administrative costs, and are backed, in most cases, by physical allocated gold.

ᵒ∫ Why a Gold ETF? ∫ᵒ

The key motivation for launching gold ETFs was to open up the gold market to a broader range of investors. One of the targets was "real money funds" (pension funds, and so on) that might have been attracted to the notion of buying gold but that previously had no route to do so, perhaps being forbidden under the terms of their mandates from owning something that could not be pigeon-holed as either a bond or an equity. Another reason is that it might be illegal for these types of institutions to have direct ownership of a commodity. Similarly, an ETF would allow retail investors a relatively simple, and cheap, avenue in which to invest in gold.

Clearly, mining shares did fall under such a potential remit of the fund industry, and they were accessible to small investors, but given the vagaries of geology, safety records, hedge books, management ability, and so on, mining shares would not necessarily have given real money direct exposure to gold.

At the time the detractors pointed out that the sheer numbers involved made it unlikely that pension funds would ever have the interest in owning gold as a diversifier to their overall portfolios. With an industry that has been estimated as having $2.6 trillion under management of defined benefit, then clearly even 1 percent would lead to some 812 tonnes of gold being bought on a basis of $1,000 as the spot gold price—something that seems unlikely given that it is about one-third of the gold that is mined each year and clearly a 1 percent holding does not count as diversification.

The first ETF for gold was launched by Gold Bullion Securities in Sydney during March 2003, followed by London Gold Bullion Securities (now LyxOr Gold Bullion Securities) nine months later, and then in a variety of other locations. However, it was only with the advent of the New York listings that volumes really accelerated.

The first and largest—there is a correlation—ETF to be launched in the United States was streetTRACKS Gold Shares, which debuted in November 2004. In May 2008, it was renamed SPDR Gold Shares, and its Web site is www.spdrgoldshares.com.

This launch was followed in January 2005 by the Comex Gold Trust (IAU). At the time of this writing (March 2010), the SPDR has over 1,116 tonnes of gold in trust, and there is a further 151 tonnes in Zurcher Kantonalbank's scheme, 118 or so tonnes in GBS UK, and 77.57 in iShares. There are currently some 18 gold ETFs, and a lot of them are really quite small. However, the total across all of them is currently in excess of 1,850 tonnes. This makes the gold ETFs the world's sixth largest holder of gold—behind the United States and Germany but ahead of China, Switzerland, and Japan.

However, a lot of these are really rather small. Figure 7-1 tracks the seven largest funds for the sake of clarity and to demonstrate the enormous customer interest that has been tapped, as can be seen in the sharply upward sloping curve. So there is little doubt that the cynics were wrong, given the rapid growth in the concept. To date the holdings have been relatively "sticky" with scant evidence of fast money rushing into, and out of, gold on price moves.

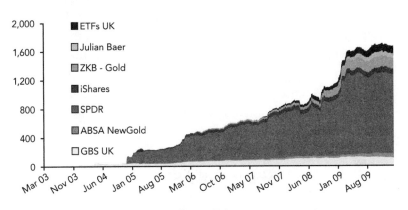

Figure 7-1

Investment in Gold Exchange-Traded Products

Source: Various exchange-traded product (ETP) issuers

⊰ Allocated Gold ⊱

Another attraction for many investors is that the ETF gold is often allocated. That is to say that the gold held by these companies is readily identifiable in the vaults by its serial numbers rather than being part of an amorphous mass. This means that the gold is the property of the fund and not a claim against the custodian (in the event that it was to go bust).

Pictures on the SPDR Web site (www.spdrgoldshares.com) show some of the gold that the company owns. SPDR notes that "Gold Shares represent fractional, undivided beneficial ownership interests in the Trust, the sole assets of which are gold bullion, and, from time to time, cash. Gold Shares are intended to lower a large number of the barriers, preventing investors from using gold as an asset allocation and trading tool. These barriers have included the logistics of buying, storing, and insuring gold. In addition, certain pension funds and mutual funds do not or cannot hold physical commodities, such as gold, or the derivatives." I have already described the barriers to ownership faced by some types of funds, but also in the paragraph preceding is the information that the shares represent beneficial ownership in the trust. Rather than owning the gold itself, the investors own a company that owns gold—the original notion that investors could own the gold itself was not practical for a number of reasons. However, this ran into both logistical and regulatory difficulties. It is difficult to argue, though, that this has in any way hampered its success.

·≡[SPDR Gold Shares]≡·

A quick glance at the press will give the latest valuation of the shares. This does not seem to correspond exactly to the gold price, which such valuations are supposed to mimic—even taking into account that they represent one-tenth of an ounce of gold. However, the definition of GLD (provided by the stock exchange) provides the answer:

Name: SPDR Gold Shares

Objective: Designed to track the price of gold (net of Trust expenses)

Symbol: GLD

Exchange: New York Stock Exchange Arca

Exchange-Traded Funds

Initial Pricing: Based on the price of 1/10 of an ounce of gold

Estimated Expense: 0.40 percent*

Minimum Order Size: 1 share

Sponsor: World Gold Trust Services, LLC

Trustee: Bank of New York

Custodian: HSBC Bank USA

Marketing Agent: State Street Global Markets, LLC, an affiliate of State Street Global Advisors

Short Sale Eligible? Yes

Margin Eligible? Yes

Structure: Continuously offered, open-ended investment trust

Thus each share will represent smaller fractions of the original one-tenth ounce of gold over time; currently (February 2010) the figure is 0.097948 of an ounce of gold. As the World Gold Council says, "The expenses of administering the GLD Trust are accrued daily so that every investor pays a fair share, and that a tiny quantity of the gold backing the shares is sold every month to meet those expenses. This means that the amount of gold backing each share is reduced over time, but it is an extremely gradual process of erosion. Full details are published on the Trust's Web site."

*The Sponsor and the Marketing Agent have agreed to reduce the fees payable to them from the assets of the Trust to the extent required so that the estimated ordinary expenses of the trust do not exceed an amount equal to 0.40 percent per annum of the daily net asset value during the period ending seven years from the date of the Trust Indenture or upon the earlier termination of the Marketing Agent Agreement. Investors should be aware that if the value of the Trust assets is less than approximately $388 million, the ordinary expenses of the Trust will be accrued at a rate greater than 0.40 percent per year of the daily ANAV of the Trust even after the Sponsor and the marketing Agent have completely reduced their combined fees of 0.30 percent per year of the daily ANAV of the Trust. This amount is based on the estimated ordinary expenses of the Trust.

While some small investors will prefer to invest via physical ownership of gold or perhaps mining equities, the simplest way is almost undoubtedly via ETFs and almost certainly why the World Gold Council (a marketing organization funded by leading mining companies; please see Appendix B, "Frequently Asked Questions") has been so active in the setting up and promotion of this investment vehicle for gold. The rationale and costs will be different for an institution.

8

Physical Gold

 For some people all gold is physical; the only type of gold that matters is the actual bars rather than the unallocated accounts and amorphous mass that are generally transacted. Therefore, in this chapter I would like to discuss *physical demand*—the generic term that market makers tend to use when they are besieged by customers asking for prices of anywhere from 500 ounces to a few thousand, usually from banks based in the Middle East and Asia but more specifically in Dubai, Hong Kong, Singapore, and so on.

For most people in the West, the notion of basing jewelry purchases—for that has traditionally been what nearly three-quarters of gold was destined to become—on the price of the metal remains rather unusual. The purchase of a wedding ring is not delayed until a suitable pullback in the price, nor is a bracelet sold because the price has rallied. However, the whole concept of gold purchases and sales has a very different connotation for much of the world.

·⟨ Lining Up to Buy Gold ⟩·

The first difference in the way that gold is viewed outside the West is the way in which the pieces themselves are displayed. Instead of price tags, each piece will carry a label that gives its fine gold content, or even gross weight and purity. In most jurisdictions the purity is likely to be at least 90 percent, rather than the 75 percent (18 carat) that is used for high-quality jewelry in the West. It is even less likely to be the 9 carat—less than 40 percent gold—that is sometimes used, and still with a label proclaiming it to be "pure 9 carat gold"—a confusion of terms in my opinion.

In Asia and the Middle East, the pieces are generally marked with the weight, and there is typically a display on the wall that has an updated gold price, the offer price, plus a small markup for manufacture and profit. If this still sounds somewhat odd, then let me use a personal anecdote to illustrate the point. When I was getting married in Hong Kong, I visited the jewelers to buy wedding rings. For my (now) wife, there was no problem as they had a ring that fit. Unfortunately they were going to have to make one for me; no problem. We went through all the usual rigmarole over size, thickness, purity, and so on. It would be ready in a week. Final question: "Do you want today's metal price, or do you want it on the day that you pick it up?" Not the sort of question that tends to get asked in Tiffany's! Being a little bullish, I opted for the former—right choice as it rallied $5 over the next seven days.

A little fatuous perhaps but true and indicative of how different the concept is in different parts of the world. I saw examples of this many times during my six years in Hong Kong. I am still astounded by the lines of buyers that I used to see form outside jewelers following sharp falls in the gold price. However, the general rule from a trading point of view is that physical demand does not kick in until the price has stabilized at lower levels, the mentality being that it can always fall further, and the demand often waits until the price has started to tick higher again.

⚜ Different Cultures, Different Rationales ⚜

Second, the rationale behind buying gold jewelry is different between cultures. From a Western perspective, jewelry is generally purchased for special occasions, with a wedding ring or engagement ring really the only time when it is considered a necessity to buy precious metals. Personally I detest going into a jewelry shop in the West, where it often seems that the attitude is that you are fortunate to be allowed in past the security gates let alone to have the temerity to inspect the pieces. A gross generalization I accept, but given my trade, I should feel extremely blasé at the process, so if it makes me feel uncomfortable, then I am sure that the feeling is magnified for a great many other people.

In Asia I have few such qualms, and the process is much more egalitarian; besides, there are any number of occasions when it is necessary to give a gift of gold. Indian wedding ceremonies are one of the most well-known examples, with the bride bedecked in gold jewelry that is her own property. It is still the case in some rural areas that the only wealth that a woman can own is her jewelry, but this used to be far more widely spread throughout Indian society.

Similarly, in Chinese society gold is given at weddings (mainly in the form of bangles) as well as occasions such as the birth of a child. Again I believe a personal anecdote can help here, as the concept seems rather alien to Western society. Both my children were born in Hong Kong.

On their birth, friends and relatives of my (Chinese) wife arrived with gifts, including gold bracelets, necklaces, and medallions, whereas the Westerners produced a succession of toys and stuffed animals. Indeed, the whole event may sound rather disproportionate, with the Chinese perhaps being overly generous. However, such is the difference in the pricing of gold jewelry between East and West that the outlay was not that dissimilar.

Admittedly the children were not exactly enthused with the gold as infants, even when it showed pigs surfing or oxen skateboarding, an attempt to make their Chinese birth symbols more relevant to a child. Indeed, there has been a growing preference for the Year of the Rat to be represented by a mouse, albeit the world's most famous mouse—Mickey. However, over 13 years later, the gold gifts are locked away safely, long after many of the toys have been thrown in the trash.

In most instances, this preference for gold has its roots locked in survival. The storage of wealth stems from a traditional need to provide for the future and to guard against tough times. Similarly to the purchase, the lack of sentimentality can be seen in the disposal of gold. Until very recently, for many in the West, every piece of jewelry was something to be treasured; the notion of trading in an old (perhaps broken) piece against the purchase of something new and more fashionable did not occur. However, the enormous publicity generated by gold as it has soared to record highs has seen attitudes change and particularly as it has coincided with a global recession. Consequently adverts for companies offering cash for gold are far more common. The notion of "scrap" is key when looking at gold data, and at its simplest it partially explains the wide gap between new supply (from mines) and demand.

Consignment Stocks

In a perfect, simple world the customer would walk into a jewelry shop intending to buy a one-ounce piece of pure gold jewelry. A quick glance at the screen would show that the shop's selling price at that particular time was $1,000. Money would change hands, and the customer would leave the store satisfied. However, the retailer would still have an outstanding short position that needed to be covered. With a quick call to his bullion bank, the retailer would buy the ounce of gold, thus locking in his profit margin.

If only. At least from the jeweler's point of view, I cannot begin to imagine the reaction of the traders I know should they be asked for prices in such small quantities. There is also the question of where the gold used in the manufacture of jewelry came from in the first place.

Instead of this overly simplistic version just described, banks will engage in their usual business of lending working capital. In this instance, the "funds" provided are in the form of gold bars rather than cash. The purities will differ for various markets and in accordance with the customary expectations of the local population and taking into account the capabilities of local jewelers. Some manufacturers need to take 9999 (four nines) kilo bars rather than 995 large bars (400 ounces) because that is the largest size their machines can process as they chop, melt, and alter the purity.

Essentially, the banks lend gold to jewelers and to manufacturers (who may not necessarily be the same entity, but let's assume that they are for greater ease). These companies then draw down the loans and pay them back (by buying gold and remitting U.S. dollars) as they see fit and depending on market circumstances. The terms of these loans will clearly vary with the creditworthiness of the customer and the overall market "tightness" (shorthand for the cost of credit, nearby interest rates, and the availability of the required bar types).

Thus a large, well-financed manufacturer might be allowed to take a consignment free of interest payments as long as the gold is to be used within a set time frame (two weeks, for example). It would repay the loan by buying the gold at the loco London spot price, plus a pre-agreed-upon premium for the bar purity, size, and location. Conversely, a small company would be given a much smaller amount of gold—perhaps even just a kilo—and would be expected to pay for a large proportion of this in advance.

Since the search for profits is eternal, the jewelers and/or manufacturers will usually try to increase their margins by trading gold, such as buying in advance of a key gift-giving season perhaps. Or if they are generally bullish or bearish about the prospects for gold, they may go long by locking in prices in advance of anticipated price increases, or conversely they may delay purchases if they believe that prices are likely to fall.

⋅≍[Gold as a Gift]≍⋅

The key gold-giving occasions are these:

Lunar New Year: The major Chinese celebration falling between late January and late February

Akshaya Thrithiya: Indian festival falling in April or May

Diwali: Start of the Indian (Hindu) New Year in October or November

Indian Wedding Season: Running from late September to late December

Eid al Fitr: Muslim festival marking the end of Ramadan

Eid al Adha: Muslim festival occurring the day after the ending of the Hajj pilgrimage

I have not given exact dates for these festivals because they are determined by lunar calendars and hence they vary from year to year. Additionally, certain other signals—mainly astrological—can count for or against the dates. For example, according to the Chinese, certain years are very propitious for getting married and/or having children. A dragon year—which happens once every 12 years—is seen as particularly lucky; thus weddings and births will surge. The converse can be true for some months during certain years; the ghost month (the seventh of the lunar year) is not particularly popular, for example.

However, while these events are key for the overall physical off-take for a given year, they will not necessarily have an impact in a given month because the retailers will look to position themselves ahead of the anticipated buying (or slowing up ahead of the ghost month), and in the case of an Indian girl, her parents may start accumulating the gold at birth rather than waiting until an announcement of marriage. Thus both buyers and sellers look to take advantage of market movements.

For all the thoughts about gold as a ready store of value, about its being a panacea in uncertain times, its greatest use still remains as jewelry—although, as per Chapter 2, the dynamics of the market have been changing with investment demand increasing at the expense of that for jewelry. However, admittedly, the notion of jewelry does vary; someone who buys a necklace at Tiffany's may have an entirely different motive from someone who buys a piece containing a similar amount of metal in Asia. Possibly it may be that the tax is different for buying adornment gold as opposed to investment metal in a particular country, and thus buying jewelry is simply much more cost-efficient than buying a small bar.

⸘ Scrap Metal ⸘

In the West, it is often felt that it is not entirely proper to sell jewelry that you have bought or been given. Indeed, generally why would you? The bracelet that you, in the West, bought for $1,000 might have only $500 of gold in it, which might be a generous estimate since markups can be anything up to 500 percent. Therefore, selling it for the scrap metal value is no way to recoup your investment. Besides, the piece was probably bought for a special occasion and now holds as much sentimental as monetary value. However, judging by the plethora of commercials, there is a concerted effort to change this Western attitude.

In contrast, and as before, there is little such sentimentality attached to the metal in other areas of the world—and swapping the jewelry for a more up to date piece makes perfect sense if the difference is only a few (not a few hundred) dollars.

Scrap is an extremely important component of the annual gold supply, second only to mining and roughly double that of official sector sales. Indeed, GFMS estimated scrap flows of 1,541 tonnes for 2009, with 501 tonnes coming from the Middle East and a further 380 tonnes from East Asia. In contrast, North America supplied just 126 tonnes of scrap gold. GFMS also noted in its publication Gold

Survey 2009 Update II, "Global scrap supply achieved a record high in 2009, rising by over 26 percent, some 900 tonnes higher than at the start of the decade."

The greatest outpouring of scrap that I ever witnessed was during the Asian financial crisis of the late 1990s. This was a period when several countries saw a meltdown in the value of their currencies. Because gold is denominated in U.S. dollars, its value in local currency terms increased substantially as regional economies were hit, dramatically underlining why the population had bought gold in the first place. To maintain purchasing power, much of this gold was then sold into the market. In some cases, national pride saw gold donated to the country to enable the hard-hit governments to sell the metal and raise much needed U.S. dollars.

9

Gold: Myths and Reality

 The task of explaining the many properties ascribed to gold to an alien would not be simple. The conversation could probably start off fairly easily, explaining that a single ounce can be drawn into 50 miles of thin gold wire or beaten into a sheet covering almost 100 square feet . . . truly remarkable.

As for its use in jewelry, because gold does not become dull and can be found as yellow, rose, or white (depending on what it is alloyed with), it is again an incredible metal. By undergoing special processes, green and purple gold can be created too.

However, trying to explain gold's role as a refuge and store of value in times of upheaval, as well as its historic inflation-busting qualities, the conversation is likely to become rather more difficult. At its worst it could degenerate into a conversation akin to one with an inquisitive six-year-old when every explanation that you flounder to give is met with the one-word answer "Why?"

⊰ History ⊱

I said at the start of the book that if anyone was interested in why the Incas had gold or the Egyptians fashioned their most valued pieces out of the metal, then this was not the right book to buy. This is where I recant very slightly, although only in passing.

The fact is that gold is an inescapable part of human history. It has been valued through millennia for its ability to shine, for its workability, and for its scarcity. In the past its use was often reserved for royalty, nobility, and items of religious significance. In some societies its color is associated with deities. This history has translated to its near mythical status over the sum of human existence.

Doubtless in the Stone Age a weapon made of stone was highly valued, whereas in the Bronze and Iron Ages it would have lost much of its value. Today few stones are seen as mythical; certainly flint is not near the top of anyone's "must have" list. However, gold has never been an everyday item, and it is this exclusivity that has been preserved throughout the ages—so much so that it is part of language and of our psyche.

At the Olympics athletes strive for gold medals, the pinnacle of achievement in their chosen sport; soccer-playing nations compete for the World Cup, made out of gold of course; winners of Nobel Prizes receive a gold medal to recognize their contribution to humankind. We acknowledge the preeminence of gold when talking about silence being "golden" or living out our "golden years." Retailers and advertisers try to cash in on this connotation by promising us "gold credit cards," "Gold Blend" coffee, "All Gold" chocolates. A quick trawl through Google for "gold and food" gives you such results as dog food, fish food, and baby food. None of them contain gold, hopefully, but it is assumed that by linking these products with gold, we will believe that we are buying a premium product and are special ourselves. Indeed, Sigmund Freud, founder of the psychoanalytic school of psychiatry, commented, "Our fascination with gold is related to the fantasies of early childhood."

⋅◦⦗ Gold as a Diversifier ⦘◦⋅

With the growth in commodities as an asset class, banks have conducted a number of studies assessing the appropriate percentage of this sector to provide the optimal Sharpe ratio for a portfolio. However, there has been little independent published research on gold in a portfolio by the largest holders of gold—the central banks.

Possibly the only publicized views have been those of the European Central Bank when it selected 15 percent in gold upon establishing the ECB (though I feel that had rather more to do with the metal ownership of its constituent members at the time) and of Maria Gueguina of the Central Bank of Russia, who, in her comments to an LBMA conference audience (covered in Chapter 3), saw 10 percent as the theoretically correct percentage of gold in that country's central bank's reserves.

The World Gold Council has commissioned a number of surveys showing the benefits that gold can bring to a portfolio. In one such study for U.S. institutional investors, called *Gold as a Strategic Asset* (Richard Michaud, Robert Michaud, and Katharine Pulvermacher, 2006), the authors concluded, "Gold may have a comparable portfolio weight to asset classes such as small cap and emerging markets due to its value as a diversifying asset. A strategic allocation to gold is dependent on portfolio risk level. We find a small though significant allocation of 1 to 2 percent at low risk and 2 to 4 percent in a balanced portfolio. While not statistically significant at high risk levels, gold may provide stability in poor markets and economic climates to long-term institutional strategic investors." See Figure 9-1. However, this rather dry statement conceals the fact that such an allocation to gold, if widespread, would cause thousands of tonnes of the metal to be bought—in a market where only some 2,500 tonnes is mined each year.

As a rough guide, taking the start of the subprime woes and the credit crunch as of August 2007, gold would have been an excellent addition to any portfolio. In that period of time, it has risen from $660 to a high of $1,210 in December 2009; and, most tellingly,

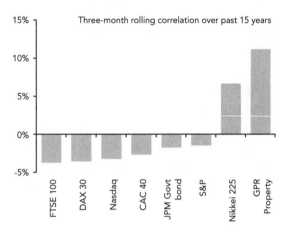

Figure 9-1
Gold's Correlation to Other Assets

Source: EcoWin and Barclays Capital

since this was not simply a result of the decline in the dollar, it rose from 485 euros to a high of 815 euros on the same day before once more rallying in terms of the European currency to a record 1,012 euros in May 2010 on widely reported debt woes of various nations in the European Union and concerns over the impact of financial contagion.

◦⟨ Gold as a Store of Value ⟩◦

Portable Wealth

This description encompasses gold's role as both a way in which it lends itself to being portable wealth and as a possible long-term hedge against inflation.

Probably the most recent example of gold representing a large-scale store of wealth is the experience of refugees during the Vietnam

War and its aftermath. Part of the population fled in leaky boats, taking their family's money with them in the form of bars, coins, and jewelry, and in some instances it was alleged that they fled with the tacit approval of the government, which allowed them to leave in the crowded vessels on payment of 10 ounces of gold per person. The metal that they were left with was intended to help them start their new lives abroad. It seems that this strategy worked reasonably well with the gold being readily convertible into cash.

By association, in the run-up to Hong Kong being handed back to China in June 1997, some comments in the international financial press suggested that the local population would be wise to convert their available assets to gold in the event that they had to take to the high seas. Living in Hong Kong at the time as I was, this was an argument that made as little sense then as it does now. I held my account with a major international bank; I knew, should the situation take a turn for the worse, rather than buy gold and look around for a small boat, I would simply ask the bank to open an account in London, New York, Tokyo, or the like, and transfer the money there for me. A few years later, I could pretty much accomplish the same thing through my online banking account.

Hong Kong is very much a first world country. This notion of gold as a store of value makes more sense in places where the banking system is not as highly developed, such as for the refugees of Darfur (if they had the money) or perhaps rural India, where a distrust of the banking system still exists.

Indeed, in the months following the Asian tsunami of December 2004, the Indian state of Tamil Nadu, one of the most urbanized regions, saw an upsurge in gold buying as survivors used their relief money to hold their savings in gold until such a time as it could be used in reconstruction.

However, as societies come to trust more in financial institutions, this feature of gold diminishes in importance. Indeed, the recent rally in the gold price was partly born out of distrust for the state of the global financial system as investors sought a safe haven for their assets, and some of the ongoing issues are encouraging people to think about maintaining a portion of their wealth in gold at all times.

The Inflation Fighter

As for inflation, there is an old anecdote that a sovereign coin (a U.K. gold coin with a metal content of just under a quarter of an ounce) has always been enough to buy dinner at the Savoy Hotel in London. Currently the Royal Mint Web site tells me that I can buy a sovereign for £230, which should buy me a very good meal. Thus, the point is proved, although not very scientifically!

If you are more fashion oriented, then perhaps the idea that an ounce of gold has always been enough to buy a respectable outfit might fit rather better. The World Gold Council has found supporting evidence of this theory by comparing the cost of clothing from medieval England (roughly, 1100 onward), through to the 1700s, and finally today ($1,000 or so being a welcome addition to the clothes budget).

Gold as a modern "inflation buster" probably dates from the gold standard because it was the mechanism whereby central banks were kept "honest" and were able to print only those notes backed by sufficient metal. Much of the evidence of the long-term historical efficacy of gold in this respect is anecdotal—as I illustrated above. However, I am going to repeat a chart that I used back in Chapter 1 because it shows the gold price plotted against the U.S. consumer price index with both of these indexed at 100 as of January 1975.

Gold has underperformed inflationary expectations over the last 20 years and perhaps arguably over the last 30 years looking at Figure 9-2. In the late 1970s and early 1980s, inflation was seen as a threat before the central bankers were thought to have reasserted control.

Perhaps controversially I believe it can be seen as a trust gap. So gold underperformed inflation when individuals, and markets,

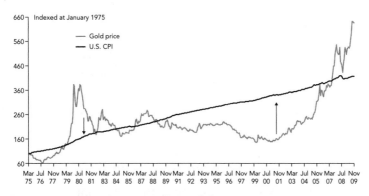

Figure 9-2

Gold's Performance Relative to U.S. Inflation

Source: EcoWin and Barclays Capital

believed that monetary authorities were in control of events and that the application of monetary policy could create an everlasting Goldilocks economy. However, from the start of the credit crunch and right through the financial crisis, these institutions have seemed to be running behind events and struggling to keep up with matters. Hence when in doubt, put your faith in gold.

The timing of gold's outperformance is significant because it coincides with gold's finding renewed favor with investors.

I believe that this trend shows that it comes down to a trust in the monetary authorities or the banking system. Trust them and you don't need gold, but if that confidence is misplaced, then these traditional attributes start to look far more attractive—just ask the residents of Tamil Nadu. This is particularly true when there are now a myriad of ways to protect oneself against inflation.

⌐ Gold Is Not a Dollar! ⌐

Several commodities can trade as a counter to the U.S. dollar, but gold is far more correlated to the currency. Briefly this is because gold is priced in dollars but often bought by the general population of other countries, such as India, China, and so on. Therefore, when the U.S. dollar falls, it is assumed that overseas investors will increase the amount that they purchase and therefore the price will go up to compensate. This could be thought of as the commodity rationale for gold's relationship to the dollar.

At least that is the theory. In reality, the rationale is generally superfluous because if the U.S. dollar falls, then gold will almost always rise—because it behaves as a currency and if the U.S. dollar drops, then gold has to rise. Gold's general under- or overperformance in terms of the U.S. dollar is perhaps rather more important since it shows its relative performance compared to extraneous influences.

Additionally, for many people gold is simply a currency, and thus if the dollar falls, gold rises in the same way that the euro, yen, or pound does. It is very simple.

The consequences of this relationship are examined in more depth in the next chapter.

ᐧᐩᐤ Conspiracy Theories ᐠᐤᐧ

With gold maintaining a hold over our psyche, it is unsurprising that it appears in so many conspiracy theories. Its anonymity and desirability only increase its mystique and hence its role in such stories and/or rumors.

In December 2000, a lawsuit was filed that alleged "manipulative activities in the gold market from 1994 to the present time orchestrated by government officials acting outside the scope of their legal or constitutional authority and certain large bullion banks active in over-the-counter gold derivatives markets and on the Commodities Exchange ("COMEX") in New York."

The defendants were a remarkable group:

1. The Bank for International Settlements (BIS), which is sometimes referred to as the "central banks' central bank"

2. Alan Greenspan, then chairman of the Board of Governors of the U.S. Federal Reserve System

3. William J. McDonough, then president of the Federal Reserve Bank of New York

4. J.P. Morgan & Co., Ltd.

5. Chase Manhattan Corp.

6. Citigroup Inc.

7. Goldman Sachs Group Inc.

8. Deutsche Bank AG

9. Lawrence H. Summers, then U.S. Secretary of the Treasury

The case was dismissed in the first quarter of 2002.

However, it seemed to be a common theme that the price of gold was languishing because of the activities of the politicians and complicit banks. The rationale for many of these was apparently that inflation was rampant, but to disguise this fact, the price of gold needed to be kept artificially low to prevent the general public from working this out. Hence, U.S. president Bill Clinton (who seemed to figure in a number of the conspiracies) apparently issued an order that gold was to be released from Fort Knox to suppress the price. Unfortunately, though, the scale of the manipulation was such that rather than being a short-term operation, where the gold could simply be bought back quickly without anyone realizing it, the stocks held in Fort Knox (in excess of 8,000 tonnes) were actually all used up.

To overcome this hurdle (clearly the gold price still needed to be kept under control), the U.S. government sought the help of the Germans who agreed to lend their entire stock of gold for this purpose. Unfortunately this was not enough to stem the bubbling undercurrent of gold demand, and the result was that a total of 11,500 tonnes of gold, nearly five years of mine supply, and $368 billion (on a basis of $1,000 per ounce) or $110 billion (on a basis of $300) were wasted in a fruitless enterprise. The net result is that the vaults of both countries are empty.

An alternative to this story was that various countries lent their gold to bullion banks that promptly sold it. The currency raised was placed on deposit, and when the gold price fell, the gold would be bought back, delivering a nice profit. Again, unfortunately, the gold price rose, leaving the banks with an enormous marked-to-market loss that threatened both the individual institutions as well as the global economy, so the matter was hushed up. Long-Term Capital Management (LTCM) often figured in this particular scenario as well.

Apparently, the European central bank Gold Agreement (EcbGA), covered in Chapter 3, was not in fact a mechanism to remove uncertainty from the price. Instead, it served to provide a degree of certainty that central banks would act in concert to ensure that the price of gold could not rally.

Any person, or institution, that disagreed with this was automatically labeled as being part of the "cabal," the group that allegedly was brought together to prevent populations from discovering that inflation was in fact rampant. In a forerunner of the "Da Vinci Code" style of conspiracy, if a matter could not be sufficiently explained, it was sometimes suggested that "the Vatican" was the mystery lender or seller of gold.

The problem, as with all the best conspiracy theories, is that such matters are hard to disprove easily. For many of the defendants, these would be nuisance allegations, not worth commenting on. Those that did bother to reply would probably content themselves with words such as "groundless" or "baseless." However, the rejoinder would probably echo the famous quip from Mandy Rice-Davies (in a real 1960s conspiracy) when she was asked why Lord Astor had denied even meeting her, let alone having had an affair: "Well, he would, wouldn't he?"

All I can say, having worked for four of the largest gold trading institutions in the world (and two of the five banks in the lawsuit mentioned above), is that I have never seen any evidence of governmental (quasi or otherwise) tampering in the gold market. I have helped many nations sell gold but have not sat on the trading desk with an enormous short position waiting for the phone to ring signaling help from the likes of President Clinton, Mr. Greenspan, Mr. Summers, or anyone else. Instead, if we had a large short position in a rising market, then it would have been with a degree of trepidation and hoping that the price fell again to enable us to at least cover our positions.

A more specific lawsuit was brought by Blanchard and Company Inc. of New Orleans—the largest retail dealer in physical gold in the United States—on behalf of themselves and their clients who had bought gold. The basic upshot of the charge was that J.P. Morgan and Barrick (the gold mining company) had colluded to suppress the price of gold at the expense of individual investors by use of its hedging program. Indeed, the allegation was that given global growth in incomes, the price should have been $740 an ounce in December 2002 rather than some $400 lower at that time.

In the end the case was settled out of court, with the charge against J.P. Morgan being dropped first and apparently Blanchard's having to pay damages to Barrick after they countersued for libel in November 2005.

Probably the foremost organization alleging manipulation of the gold price is GATA, which describes itself on its Web site (www. gata.org) as the "Gold Anti-Trust Action Committee . . . organized in January 1999 to advocate and undertake litigation against illegal collusion to control the price and supply of gold and related financial securities." Despite the recent rise in gold to all-time record (nominal) highs, GATA believes that gold is still undervalued. In a full-page advertisement taken out in the *Wall Street Journal* in January 2008, it stated, among other things, that "the gold reserves of the United States have not been fully and independently audited for half a century. Now there is proof that those gold reserves and those of other Western nations are being used for the surreptitious manipulation of the international currency, commodity, equity, and bond markets. . . .

"The objective of this manipulation is to conceal the mismanagement of the U.S. dollar so that it might retain its function as the world's reserve currency. But to suppress the price of gold is to disable the barometer of the international financial system so that all markets may be more easily manipulated. This manipulation has been a primary cause of the catastrophic excesses in the markets that now threaten the whole world.

"Gold's recent rise toward $900 per ounce shows that the price-suppression scheme is faltering. When it is widely understood how central banks have been suppressing gold, its price may rise to $3,000 or $5,000 or more."

The argument seems to have moved on from just the Clinton administration "manipulating" the gold price to a general concern about central banks and governments as a whole. I have met with 45 out of the world's 50 largest holders of gold in their own countries and have discussed the topic of gold reserve management with almost all 50 of these nations. Not once have I ever been asked how to prevent the rise of the price of gold. Not once have I ever had a discussion on gold being the bellwether of world financial health and how keeping the price low will bring benefits in other markets. Not once have I seen large gold orders placed by central banks to act as a lid on the gold price.

However, I have had many conversations on the most effective way to sell gold and to minimize market disruption. I have sat with political and financial leaders who believe that selling gold would be akin to disposing of a family heirloom. I have heard a senior central banker bemoaning that the low yields obtainable on gold reserves means that the central bank needs funds from the ministry of finance just to meet its running costs—politically very unpopular—and elsewhere was told by a central bank governor that even discussing mobilizing gold reserves could be enough to bring the government down.

So, yes, gold is sensitive; it is seen as a case entirely different from that of any other reserve asset—but is there a conspiracy? I think not. In fact, I know not.

⫷ Gold the Barometer ⫸

I do find myself agreeing with GATA, though, that gold can be a barometer of the global financial health. Whereas it could have been argued for much of the 1990s, and indeed for much of this millennium, that gold had lost its place as a major financial instrument, the recent turmoil in the currency and fixed income markets has rekindled interest in the metal as an investment and as an important financial instrument. As I noted earlier in this book, the events of the last 30 years were perhaps an aberration in our relationship with gold which has lasted for millennia.

In the next chapter I investigate how to get exposure to gold.

10

Getting Exposure to Gold

Hopefully you are now armed with enough information to try to interpret what is going on in the gold market: whether traders are slavishly following the fortunes of the U.S. dollar, or whether perhaps gold is moving without regard to other markets (how the metal is faring against the euro). Is it a wider commodities rally? Is gold acting as a diversifier? What is going on in the global economy? Have there been any pronouncements recently from central banks or sovereign wealth funds? Perhaps even more importantly, what is the state of the world? How are monetary authorities viewed? What is the risk of contagion? Can the market shrug off bad news?

All of these added together come up with the most important dynamic of all—sentiment. Clearly doing the homework by asking questions like these is always going to be crucial, but even more so if the position is taken to use gold as an outright long trade rather than using it as a portfolio diversifier. In the latter case, the general assumption is that just about any time is going to make sense.

Before running through the various alternatives, I have to admit that I am not a financial advisor. I deal with large financial institutions that operate complex risk evaluation systems and that are required to undergo all sorts of checks before I am even allowed to talk to them. The rationale for any trade might be completely different for small companies and private individuals where the motivation, and risk appetite, could be based on totally divergent criteria; in that case, it obviously makes sense to consult a financial advisor who clearly understands the relevant needs and potential risks before entering into any such trades. Indeed, in jurisdictions like the United Kingdom, I am simply not allowed by law to talk to private individuals about gold.

Equities

If you are convinced that it is appropriate to take a position in gold, then how should you go about it? Via physical, futures, ETFs, or mining shares? Personally I know nothing about equities so I am not going to even bother to try to explain them. However, if you were to buy a junior explorer that discovered some enormous untapped seam, then it would seem likely that you would end up making far more money than if you were simply long gold. The problem is finding this miracle stock. Alternatively, you might be long via one of the large mining companies as a closer proxy to the gold price; but then what is going to make this company outperform, and what happens if the gold price rallies because this mining company has had to shut a mine because of safety concerns? Potentially you would have the right position—gold rallied; but you would be in the wrong place as your shares went down. All of this seems to be rather complicated to me unless you know the sector extremely well.

Physical

There is always the direct route. If you are bullish for gold, then what could be more practical than actually owning a lump of it? Should the global economy start to fall apart, you have the ultimate insurance, an investment outside of the usual financial world, assuming that you keep your investment somewhere safe. If you had kept a safe deposit box at Northern Rock (a British savings institution that experienced a run on it during 2007), then you would have been lining up outside with everyone else desperate to ensure that your "money" was safe—despite this investment being segregated from the bank itself, the natural reaction would have been to check that it was indeed so. Of course you could open an account with a "too-big-to fail" institution (if there is such a thing), but it does somewhat take away from the rationale that sparked the decision to buy and particularly the decision to buy physical. Instead, then, do you keep it at home? Do you buy a safe to store it in? What about general security? What happens if you get robbed?

These questions do not even take into consideration such concerns as the tax regime of where you live. Is there a goods and services tax payable? Is it reclaimable once you sell it? Perhaps even more importantly, what is the markup? How much is the retailer going to charge you over the loco London price? Obviously you are not going to march into Tiffany's to buy a chain with 5 ounces of gold in it, but what is the premium that you are paying, and are you better off buying Canadian maples, Australian nuggets, Chinese pandas, Austrian philharmonikers, or any of the plethora of other bullion gold coins that exist? Is it worth considering gold coins that have a numismatic value? Probably not, if you want exposure to the gold price rather than introducing issues such as provenance, condition, and so on. However, this is another field I know little about, and it seems to have the potential for introducing more variables when all the investor craves is simplicity.

Or is perhaps buying a few small bars a better idea? It is worth noting that, as a general rule, the smaller the bar or coin, the greater the premium that you will end up paying.

·⫶ Futures ⫶·

If you are not concerned that the world financial system is in imminent danger of folding, then you may well be better off by getting exposure to gold via futures, unallocated gold, or ETFs. If your rationale is to take a simple short-term trading position, then, depending on the size of investment, you could well be better off by trading in the futures markets. Most likely you would do so in your own currency, but if you just want a large liquid exchange, then most people would probably look to the U.S. market and particularly the CME Globex electronic trading system. These venues allow for quick movements in and out of positions anonymously, but they may be more of a problem for larger investors or traders as the liquidity is often better in OTC markets than in the futures market.

However, if, rather than trading gold, the motive is for a long-term holding, and perhaps diversification, then futures are a rather more cumbersome way of expressing this view. Which contract month do you want to go long of? Each time the month becomes due, the position then needs to be rolled into the next active period, and so on—not disastrous, but just a little inconvenient.

·⊲| Unallocated Gold |⊳·

Having an unallocated account with a bank is a simple way of trading in gold; in fact, it is very similar to any other account that you might hold with a bank. Statements will arrive showing your particular balance; a simple phone call to the institution will allow you to add to this or indeed to reduce it—all very neat. However, the problem is that normally trading rooms are set up to deal with large institutions such as other banks, hedge funds, sovereign wealth funds, central banks, and pension funds. They also tend to impose rules regarding the minimum sizes of trades, perhaps 1,000 ounces of gold and 50,000 ounces of silver. They also may not have time to discuss the vagaries of the prevailing market, unless you are a very large volume customer. Indeed, in many jurisdictions, staff members in trading rooms are forbidden by law to talk to private individuals and can converse only with other market professionals; this rule is to ensure that the general public is served by people who have a better understanding of their risk profile.

Indeed, a conversation on gold I might have with a hedge fund, at its briefest, might simply be this:

Hedge Fund: Gold in 20k.

Banker: 20–70.

Hedge Fund: At 70.

Banker: Done.

The entire process lasts less than 15 seconds.

The translation of this conversation is this:

Hedge Fund: Spot gold in 20,000 ounces, please.

Banker: I would buy at $1,100.20 per ounce troy and sell at $1,100.70 per troy ounce of loco London gold.

Hedge Fund: I buy 20,000 ounces.

Banker: Agreed; we sell you 20,000 ounces of spot gold at $1,100.70 delivery to your clearing account in London.

So ultimately it is very likely that private individuals will end up by dealing through their private banker or local branch, and even then the business might not meet the minimum size requirements.

In effect, trading directly with the various bullion banks is an option open only to large institutions or professional investors. These large institutions can also choose to hold gold in allocated form.

⊰ Allocated Gold ⊱

I have referred to this earlier in the book, but an allocated gold account is one in which the gold that an investor owns is ring-fenced from the credit of the institution where it is stored. Theoretically you can visit a vault and see your own gold bars stored separately from the general mass of metal, although, understandably enough, "vault voyeurism" is not encouraged. Given that the standard unit of trading is the 400-ounce bar (with a value of $400,000 at a price of $1,000), then it is clearly an option open only to the superrich or to large money managers. Generally it is cheaper than holding gold in an ETF—which offers much the same comfort—which is why a number of institutions have publicly described switching to allocated gold. However, for private individuals there is little doubt that the ETF is a much easier and more manageable way to hold gold.

⇥ Exchange-Traded Funds ⇤

There is an additional case for ETFs, and that is that they are essentially just shares. If an investor is looking to buy gold for diversification, then clearly there is a portfolio that needs to be diversified. Obviously it is likely to contain at least some equities, and therefore the individual is likely to already have a relationship with a stockbroker or someone in a similar position. In that case, the gold ETF can simply be added via this route. Because the ETF is effectively only one-tenth of an ounce of gold, it can accommodate small purchases, and there is easy freedom of movement, with no concerns over security, goods and services taxes, and so on. Also, since it is relatively easy for trading houses to arbitrage between loco London and the ETF, it is likely to always track the gold price closely. Therefore, it seems that the only real issues for investors are the charges levied and whether the company backing the scheme is creditworthy.

A romantic notion of the ETF was that each investor would own a percentage of a specific gold bar directly. Thus, in theory, the investors could have marched into the custodians' place of business and demanded to see their bars. In practice, the custodians would never have allowed investors to do this, of course, because banks generally do not like the general public knowing where large quantities of gold are stored, and they certainly would not have taken investors on guided tours. (However, the Federal Reserve Bank of New York is an honorable exception that does indeed allow visitors to their vaults; for details, see its Web site, www.newyorkfed.org.)

Anyway, the actual problem with ETFs is the impossible logistics: you might want to sell your portion of a gold bar, but what about the other people who own the other bits of the bar? Therefore, instead of owning the gold itself, you end up owning shares in a trust whose only asset is gold. Not quite the same thing for some people, but ETFs have been an astounding success and have created a whole new class of investors.

◦◦[Structured Notes]◦◦

For investors who require a different type of product but still want exposure to the gold price, there are various structured notes for them to invest in. The following two ideas are from Barclays Capital Commodity Investor Solutions, and their purpose here is just to give an idea of the types of trades that investors have been looking at. Obviously, as with all pricing in this book, the levels are indicative and purely for illustration; in neither of the two examples that follow does the investor actually own gold, but instead the investor is exposed to a structure where the return is based on the performance of gold.

Both of these types of structured notes are capital guaranteed, so in return for no downside, should the gold price move lower, there is no conventional full participation in the upside. However, because the second structure has a floating strike call, it is possible to benefit even if gold is at the same price, or even if it is lower, at the end of two years as it was at the start.

The first structure is a two-year note with 28 percent participation on a gold rally. If at maturity gold is up by 40 percent, the client receives 40 percent times 28 percent, or 11.5 percent. If gold is down at maturity, there is no payoff, but no capital is lost. Obviously, it is simple to understand and to see the trade-off between no loss if gold goes lower but only limited participation as it rallies.

The second, rather more esoteric structure rejoices under the name of the floating shark fin note. It is called a "shark fin" because the call option can knock out if gold ever increases by 45 percent of its initial price (continuous observation). In other words, the yield can go up steeply but plummet if gold rallies 45 percent from its starting price; then the final return would be zero, although the principal would still be protected.

As above, the call is a floating strike being determined as the lowest price observed during the two-year period of the note according to a specified strike schedule. For example, if gold ever trades below $900, it will be $900; and if it ever trades below $850, the strike will be $850; if it ever trades below $800, the strike will be $800; and so on.

If at maturity gold is up by 40 percent from the set strike, then the investor receives a 40 percent return (compared to 11.5 percent with the standard bull note above). Even if gold has fallen over the period, then it is still possible to make money because the strike will be lower.

For example: On the trade date gold is $935 per ounce. At some point during the two years, it falls below $800 (and the floating strike call is set there). Then, at maturity gold is trading at $900. The investor would make [(900/800) − 1] percent = 12.5 percent. Under the standard bull note, the yield would be zero.

However—and this is a big however—should gold rally and ever trade, during the two-year duration of this structure, above $1,350 [$935 + (45% × $935) in this example], then at maturity the investor would simply receive his or her principal back.

⌐⊏ Conclusion ⊐⌐

The environment for gold has changed enormously over the last few years. The resurgence of inflation as a potential threat, the lessening of confidence in the financial system as both banks and the monetary authorities have shown themselves struggling to contain events, uncertainty over the worth of sovereign debt, the weaker dollar, and the emergence of gold and commodities as a reinvigorated asset class have all added to the positive sentiment that surrounds gold.

Getting Exposure to Gold

Should investors (and the investors' advisors) decide that gold suits their portfolio, then there are a great number of ways in which to take advantage of this. The course of action will depend on risk profile and circumstances, but the investment could be via physical gold, some form of gold-backed note, or simply, and perhaps most suitably in my view, via the ETF.

However, whatever the ultimate route, it seems unlikely that gold will relinquish the opportunity to once again be a significant feature in global financial markets.

"Rules" for Trading Gold

 Obviously these rules are nothing more than personal opinion and are just a short checklist to bear in mind. The final point is somewhat tongue in cheek!

1. What is your motivation: diversification or appreciation?

2. For what time frame are you considering holding gold?

3. What is your view of the U.S. dollar?

4. How has gold performed against the euro and other currencies?

5. What is the geopolitical picture?

6. What is the market sentiment?

7. How much attention is gold receiving?

8. Have central banks or sovereign wealth funds announced plans?

9. Take a look at the charts.

10. Do you want allocated or unallocated metal?

11. Never trust silver!

Silver trades very differently from gold and is generally far more volatile. It has even fewer fundamentals of its own than gold, and some 70 percent of its production is a by-product of mining other metals. Silver also tends to attract highly speculative money that wants to get involved in precious metals but considers gold to be too expensive.

Nevertheless, trading the gold/silver ratio is quite a common practice. Generally silver will move more dramatically than gold; so it can work to buy silver and sell gold (in a bullish environment for gold)—that is, sell the ratio, and do the opposite where gold is considered to be in a bear market (Figure A-1). However, much of the effectiveness of this trade will depend on the relative level of the prices at inception.

That all may sound counterintuitive, but it is simply that silver will tend to exaggerate price moves in gold.

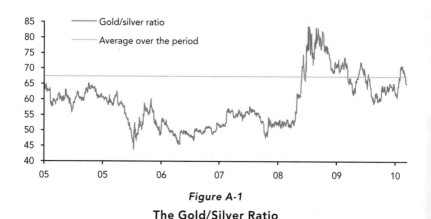

Figure A-1
The Gold/Silver Ratio

Source: EcoWin and Barclays Capital

Frequently Asked Questions

1. How much gold has ever been mined?

   By the end of "2008 total above-ground stocks, by definition cumulative historical mine production, totaled 163,000 tonnes, up 1.5 percent year-on-year." (Data from GFMS Gold Survey 2009.)

2. Which country produces the most gold?

   In 2008 it was China with 292.0 tonnes, followed by the United States at 234.5, South Africa at 233.3, and Australia at 215.2 tonnes. (Data from GFMS Gold Survey 2009.)

3. Which is the world's largest gold mining company?

   Barrick Gold, which produced 238.3 tonnes in 2008, down from 250.7 tonnes a year earlier.

4. How much gold is mined each year?

   2,415.6 tonnes of gold were mined globally in 2008, which was down from 2,478.0 tonnes a year earlier. For comparison the equivalent figure in 2000 was 2,618. (Data from GFMS Gold Survey 2009.)

5. What is the production cost for gold?

   Miners' cash costs for the first nine months of 2009 were $469 per ounce. Total production costs for the same period were $601. (Data from GFMS Gold Survey 2009.)

6. What is the world's deepest gold mine?

   It is Anglogold Ashanti's Mponeng mine, which is located just outside Johannesburg and is an impressive 3,778 meters (a little under 2½ miles) deep. (Data from Virtual Metals Group.) According to my colleague, Martyn Whitehead, who worked at a number of Anglogold mines, you travel down three separate shafts to get that deep, and it takes over an hour to get there.

7. What is the world's most productive mine?

   In 2008 the largest primary gold mine was Newmont's Nevada gold mine (2.26 million ounces, or 70.6 tonnes) although Freeport-McMoRan Grasberg mine in Indonesia, which is also a copper mine, in some years has a larger output. (Data from Virtual Metals Group.)

8. Which country consumes the most gold—essentially jewelry?

   India consumed 474.6 tonnes of gold jewelry in 2008, with China in second place at 326.7 tonnes. The United States came in third with 179.1. (Data from GFMS Gold Survey 2009.)

9. What is the biggest use of gold?

   Jewelry consumption—in 2008 it was 2,125.8 tonnes, down from 3,204 tonnes in 2000. (Data from GFMS Gold Survey 2009.)

10. What is the "identifiable investment" for gold?

    In 2008 this reached 927 tonnes, up from 165 tonnes in 2000. (Data from GFMS Gold Survey 2009.)

Frequently Asked Questions

11. What is the supply/demand balance?

    In 2008 it was 3,880 tonnes, down from 4,017 tonnes in 2000. Supply, apart from mine supply, is from official sector sales (246 tonnes) and gold scrap (1,218 tonnes). (Data from GFMS Gold Survey 2008.)

12. How much gold do central banks hold?

    Some 30,000 or so tonnes. It is difficult to get exact figures as it is claimed that there is both under- and overreporting in the International Monetary Fund (IMF) statistics. Additionally, balances will change as the central banks buy and sell gold.

13. Which country holds the most gold?

    The United States has the world's largest gold reserves, holding 8,133.50 tonnes. At a price of $1,120 this amount would be worth in excess of $291.5 billion (8,133.5 × 32,000 × 1,120). However, if the United States decided it was going to sell its gold, then the price would be significantly lower—very quickly!

14. Where do central banks hold their gold?

    The vast majority of central banks hold their gold in allocated form. Some might be held in their own vaults, some might be in the Federal Reserve Bank in New York. However, any central bank that wants to trade its gold must hold it in the Bank of England (if in allocated form) because the Bank of England's vaults are in London and metal held there can be easily moved in and out of the clearing system.

    Still, it is extremely easy to defer delivery and allow time to ship the gold. In certain transactions a central bank might lend gold loco the Federal Reserve Bank in New York and receive it back at the Bank of England in London. Or it might simply sell it loco New York, leaving the bullion bank to make the shipping arrangements.

15. What is the WGC?

"The World Gold Council's mission is to stimulate and sustain the demand for gold and to create enduring value for its stakeholders. The organisation represents the world's leading gold mining companies, who produce more than 60% of the world's annual corporate gold production in a responsible manner and whose Chairmen and CEOs form the Board of the World Gold Council (WGC).

"As the gold industry's key market development body, WGC works with multiple partners to create structural shifts in demand and to promote the use of gold in all its forms; as an investment by opening new market channels and making gold's wealth preservation qualities better understood; in jewellery through the development of the premium market and the protection of the mass market; in industry through the development of the electronics market and the support of emerging technologies; and in government affairs through engagement in macro-economic policy issues, lowering regulatory barriers to gold ownership and the promotion of gold as a reserve asset.

"The WGC is a commercially driven organisation and is focussed on creating a new prominence for gold. It has its headquarters in London and operations in the key gold demand centres of India, China, the Middle East, and United States. The WGC is the leading source of independent research and knowledge on the international gold market and on gold's role in meeting the social and economic demands of society."

Its Web site is www.gold.org.

16. What is GFMS?

According to the GFMS Web site, "GFMS is the world's foremost precious metals consultancy, specializing in research into the global gold, silver, platinum, and palladium markets. GFMS is based in London, U.K., but has representation in Australia, India, China, Germany, France, Spain, and

Russia, and a vast range of contacts and associates across the world. Our research team of fifteen full-time analysts comprises qualified and experienced economists and geologists; while two consultants contribute insights on important regional markets." Its Web site is www.gfms.co.uk.

17. What is Virtual Metals?

"*Established in 1997 and expanded in 2001, the VM Group is an independent commodities research consultancy covering precious and base metals, energy, and agricommodities. VMG specializes in macro-economic analysis of these commodities, both of the fundamentals, through generation of supply and demand scenarios, and in-depth understanding of related investment and derivatives markets. Using this analysis we derive for our clients price forecasts, projections concerning future supply/demand, and strategic recommendations.*

"*Through VMG's collaboration with Fortis Bank Nederland, the company offers a full range of independent and comprehensive publications in commodity markets that are available on a complimentary basis."* For more information contact info@vmgroup.co.uk.

18. What is the LBMA?

"*The LBMA is the London-based trade association that represents the wholesale gold and silver bullion market in London. London is the focus of the international Over-the-Counter (OTC) market for gold and silver, with a client base that includes the majority of the central banks that hold gold, plus producers, refiners, fabricators, and other traders throughout the world. The LBMA was formally incorporated in 1987 in close consultation with the Bank of England.*

"*The LBMA Good Delivery List is now widely recognized as representing the de facto standard for the quality of gold and silver bars, in large part thanks to the stringent criteria for assaying standards and bar quality that an applicant must satisfy in order to be listed. The assaying capabilities of refiners on the Good Delivery List are periodically checked under the LBMA's Proactive Monitoring program.*

"The ongoing work of the Association encompasses many areas, among them refining standards, trading documentation, and the fostering of good trading practices. Some examples:

- *In the refining industry, the LBMA Good Delivery List is widely recognized as representing the de facto standard for the quality of gold and silver bars, in large part thanks to the stringent criteria that an applicant must satisfy before being listed. In January 2004 the LBMA introduced proactive monitoring of refiners on the List, an important initiative which further enhances the reputation of the List and the refiners on it.*

- *In conjunction with the foreign exchange and money markets in London, the Association has developed the Non-Investment Products Code, which provides a code of conduct by which all Members and Associates are required to abide.*

- *The LBMA's annual Precious Metals Conference is now the premier professional forum for the world's bullion market."*

The LBMA Web site is www.lbma.org.uk.

19. Does gold have an interest rate?

Contrary to many people's expectations, it does. However, there is no central authority looking to set rates. Instead, it is simply a question of supply and demand. Traditionally the vast majority of supply has been from central banks, and the demand has been from gold mining companies for hedging purposes. In the almost total absence of hedging, gold interest rates have sunk and the metal yields very little: only around 1 basis point (0.01 percent) for one month and just 60 basis points (0.6 percent) for 10 years on a semiannual basis.

20. What is GOFO?

    GOFO is a corruption of GOld FOrward, and it is the Reuters page where gold lending rates, on a swap basis, are published every day.

21. What does the price of gold in the newspaper mean?

    Obviously it will vary from country to country, but if it is in dollars and does not give a month indication next to it, then it is likely to be the spot price for a troy ounce of loco London unallocated gold.

22. What is the "standard" price for gold?

    The loco London spot price is the standard. Gold to be delivered in any other location or purity or bar size will be quoted as a premium or discount to this price.

23. Is there a benchmark price for gold?

    The London gold fixing is universally accepted as the benchmark price. This takes place twice each day at 10.30 a.m. and 3 p.m. London time. From time to time there is a debate about whether either of these two fixings is more representative than the other. In my opinion they are equally valid, although it is occasionally argued that the afternoon fixing is more important as it takes place when both London and New York are open for business.

24. What does loco London mean?

    Gold settles over accounts in London in the same way that U.S. dollars do in New York or Japanese yen in Tokyo. As such, gold is loco London, and dollars are loco New York, and yen loco Tokyo although the terminology isn't used in these markets.

25. What is a loco swap?

A loco swap is an agreement to exchange equivalent quantities of gold in two separate locations. One location will almost invariably be London, but the other could be a variety of places such as Zurich, Germiston (at the Rand Refinery just outside Johannesburg, South Africa), the Federal Reserve in New York, and so on.

The trade is booked as the purchase of gold in one location and the sale of an equivalent amount in the other. The price differential will be a reflection of the demand for gold in each location, but at its simplest it may be nothing more than the cost of shipping the metal into London, plus refining costs if necessary.

26. What is a troy ounce?

The troy ounce is the standard unit of measurement for gold. In everyday life we use avoirdupois ounces, which are smaller than troy ounces, or ounces troy, which is the correct terminology but which is almost never used. The term troy is thought to originate from a medieval gold fair that was held in the French town of Troies. A troy ounce is 1.09714 standard ounces.

27. What is a London Good Delivery bar?

The London Bullion Market Association (LBMA) sets the definitions as follows: "The physical settlement of a loco London gold trade is a bar conforming to the following specifications:

***Weight: Minimum Gold Content:** 350 fine troy ounces (approximately 10.9 kilograms)*
***Maximum Gold Content:** 430 fine troy ounces (approximately 13.4 kilograms)*

The gross weight of a bar should be expressed in troy ounces, in multiples of 0.025, rounded down to the nearest 0.025 of a troy ounce.

Dimensions: *The recommended dimensions for a Good Delivery gold bar are approximately as follows:*

Length (Top): *250 mm ± 40 mm Undercut:* *7 percent to 15 percent*

Width (Top): *70 mm ± 15 mm Undercut: 15 percent to 30 percent*

Height: *35 mm ± 10 mm*

Fineness: *The minimum acceptable fineness is 995.0 parts per thousand fine gold. Additionally, each bar has to have a serial number, the stamp of the refiner, year of manufacture, and fineness of gold to four significant figures.*

28. What is contango?

   The gold market is almost invariably "in contango." This means that the forward price—the price for delivery of gold further ahead than two business days—is higher than the spot price. This gap is to account for the relative differences in gold and U.S. dollar interest rates, with the latter normally higher than the former.

29. What is backwardation?

   More traditional commodities have generally tended to be in backwardation—the exact reverse of contango—to reflect their relative scarcity and the need of companies to use them in manufacturing, and so on. Thus the prices "further down the curve," which means for delivery at a later date, are lower than those for immediate delivery.

*The undercut refers to the degree of slope on the side and ends of the bar, and it is calculated by deducting the dimension of the bottom edge of the bar from the dimension of the top edge and dividing the result by the top edge dimension multiplied by 100 to obtain the percentage undercut.

30. What are the main trading centers for gold?

    For Asia they are Sydney, Singapore, Hong Kong, and Tokyo. For Europe they are London and Zurich. For the Americas it is New York.

31. How many market makers are there in gold?

    It depends on who you are and what you do. However, in each trading center there are no more than nine interbank market makers—that is, institutions that are obligated to make two-way prices to each other. However, there will be many other institutions that will make markets to their customers.

32. Which group is the most influential in the gold market?

    Without a doubt it used to be the gold mining companies via their hedging programs, and then when they unwound their hedge books. However, it is probably now the hedge funds, both when gold was a version of the "carry trade" and more recently when gold has been a favored tool to express an economic view. Central banks are also clearly important, when announcing a sale or purchase, but generally their influence does not impact the gold market on a day-to-day basis. Indeed, all the central banks that I have ever talked to on gold (probably some 60 or so) do not want to impact the market in any way.

33. What are allocated and unallocated gold?

    If you hold allocated gold on account, then you know exactly which bars you own. Indeed, your statement will list each bar, its gross weight, fineness (purity), and net weight. If you have an unallocated account, then it will simply list the amount of gold that you own.

    My favorite analogy is the difference between having a safe deposit box and a checking account. In the same way that the majority of us have checking accounts rather than safe deposit boxes, the same is true for participants in the gold market; unallocated gold is the more typical form of ownership.

34. Is the gold market regulated?

   This will vary by jurisdiction, but as a general guide, trading on exchange or by other forms of derivative is more likely to be subject to regulation in a particular country. In the United Kingdom, for example, it is the Financial Services Authority (FSA) that has responsibility for regulated activities. In the United States, the New York Mercantile Exchange (NYME) is regulated by the Commodity Futures Trading Commission (CFTC), and exchange-traded notes are traded on exchanges such as the New York Stock Exchange (NYSE), which are regulated by the Securities and Exchange Commission (SEC).

35. What is the EcbGA?

   It stands for European central bank Gold Agreement. The bizarre mixture of upper- and lowercase letters is supposed to represent that it is an agreement by European central banks rather than by the European Central Bank (the Frankfurt-based institution that is the main central bank for countries that have the euro as their currency and is responsible for setting interest rates among other things). The original agreement was signed on September 26, 1999, and it ran for five years over which its 15 signatories limited themselves to selling 2,000 tonnes of gold and no more than 400 tonnes in any quota year (which begins on September 27 and continues through the following September 26). The follow-up, also for five years, increased the amount to 2,500 tonnes and no more than 500 in any quota year. The current agreement (which runs from September 2009 until 2014) reduced the total back to 2,000 tonnes and the maximum in any quota year to 400 tonnes.

36. Is there a conspiracy to manipulate the gold price?

   I have worked at four banks—Credit Suisse, Chase Manhattan, Deutsche Bank, and Barclays Bank. These are some of the world's most important "bullion banks," and all were market makers when I worked for them. In my near

27 years in these markets, I have never seen evidence of any conspiracy, and indeed the overwhelming attitude of central banks has been to take a low profile within the market. For the avoidance of doubt, I have never met anyone working in the precious metals division of a major bank who believes in such conspiracy theories.

37. What is GATA?

GATA notes that "[the] Gold Anti-Trust Action Committee was organized in January 1999 to advocate and undertake litigation against illegal collusion to control the price and supply of gold and related financial securities." The committee's Web site is www.gata.org.

38. What is No Dirty Gold?

No Dirty Gold describes itself as not seeking to boycott gold or metals but rather supporting efforts to "promote responsible mining practices and phase out irresponsible practices. . . . Thus far, more than 30 major jewelry retailers have endorsed the No Dirty Gold campaign's criteria for more responsible mining— also known as 'The Golden Rules.' These retailers, including such major corporations as Signet in the United Kingdom, Tiffany & Co. and Walmart in the United States, and Cartier/ Richemont in Europe, have also committed to sourcing gold and precious metals from operations that meet these social and environmental criteria. In 2006, a multi-stakeholder initiative (including NGOs like Earthworks and Oxfam America, jewelry retailers, mining companies, labor unions, and mining-affected communities) called IRMA was launched, with the objective of developing a system for independent verification of compliance with environmental and social standards for mining operations.

"No Dirty Gold has also helped to spur the development of CRJP, the Council for Responsible Jewelry Practices (an

association of mining and jewelry companies promoting greater corporate responsibility among its members)." For more information see www.nodirtygold.org/supporting_retailers.cfm, www.responsiblemining.net, and www.responsiblejewellery.com.

39. What is ARM?

ARM calls itself "an independent, global-scale effort, and pioneer initiative, created as an international and multi-institutional organization to bring credibility, transparency, and legitimacy to the development of a framework for responsible artisanal and small-scale mining." It is also looking to consumers to change their habits by educating "consumers as to their power to directly improve the quality of life of artisanal miners by purchasing fair trade jewelry and minerals." The ARM Web site is www.communitymining.org.

Glossary of Terms

(This glossary is provided courtesy of the London Bullion Market Association and the London Platinum and Palladium Market.)

Accelerated Supply: Precious metal sold to the market before it is physically produced—generally created by producer hedging or finance transactions.

Aliquot: A small representative sample taken from a precious metals bar for assay to determine its fine precious metals content.

Allocated Accounts: These accounts are opened when a customer requires metal to be physically segregated and needs a detailed list of weights and assays.

Alloy: A mixture of two or more chemical elements, including at least one metal. In the case of gold, it is mixed with a baser metal or metals to lower the purity, influence the color, or add durability.

American-Style Option: An option that can be exercised at any stage during its life, at or before expiration date.

Arbitrage: Simultaneous buying and selling of the same asset in different markets in order to capitalize on variations in price between those markets.

Asian-Style Option: An option that, if it expires in-the-money, is automatically settled on the basis of the difference between the strike price and the average price of the underlying asset in a given period prior to expiration.

Ask: The price a dealer or seller asks for a commodity.

Assay: The determination of the precious metal content of an alloy, either using a direct method (where the actual precious metal content is measured) or an indirect, instrumental method (usually based on spectrographic analysis) in which the levels of impurities are measured and the precious metal content is calculated by difference. For gold, the main direct method is fire assay, also known as cupellation or gravimetric analysis.

Assayer: A tester of precious metals.

Assay Mark: The stamp by an assayer on a bar or piece of precious metal to guarantee its fineness.

Assay Office: An official or statutory organization controlling the testing of precious metals within a country.

At the Money: Refers to an option strike price that is equal to the current market price of the underlying asset.

Australian Securities Exchange: The ASX was formed in 2006 following the merger of the Sydney Futures Exchange with the Australian Stock Exchange. Web site: www.asx.com.au.

Average Strike Options: Asian-style options where the ultimate settlement depends on an average strike price rather than an average underlying asset price.

Averaging: A method whereby a smoothing of the fluctuations in price movements may be achieved by agreeing to buy or sell a specified total quantity of precious metal on the basis of average prices over an agreed period of time.

Backwardation: A market situation where prices for future delivery are lower than the spot price, caused by shortage or tightness of supply.

Bank of England: Founded in 1694, "The Old Lady of Threadneedle Street" has been the focal point of gold and silver trading in London for over three centuries. It is one of the most active central banks in gold and is the gold depository for many of the world's central banks. Web site: www.bankofengland.co.uk.

Bar Chart: A type of chart commonly used in technical analysis that shows highs, lows, and closing prices.

Barrier Options: Exotic options that either come to life (are knocked-in) or are extinguished (knocked-out) under conditions stipulated in the options contract. The conditions are usually defined in terms of a price level (barrier, knock-out, or knock-in price) that may be reached at any time during the lifetime of the option. There are four major types of barrier options: up-and-out, up-and-in, down-and-out, and down-and-in. The extinguishing or activating features of these options mean that they are usually cheaper than ordinary options, making them attractive to purchasers looking to avoid high premium.

Bear: Someone who expects prices to fall.

Bear Call Spread: The purchase and sale of call options at different exercise prices but with the same expiry date. The purchased (or long) calls have a higher exercise price than the written (or short) calls. The investor expects a fall in the price of the underlying asset.

Bear Market: A market in which the trend is for prices to decline.

Bear Put Spread: The purchase and sale of put options at different exercise prices but with the same expiry date. The puts purchased have a higher exercise price than the puts written. The investor expects a fall in the price of the underlying asset.

Bermuda-Style Option: Exotic options that combine certain features of American- and European-style options. They may be exercised on predetermined dates during the lifetime of the option or on the expiry date. (*See also* American-Style Option and European-Style Option.)

Beta: The beta of a rate or price is the extent to which that rate or price follows movements in the overall market. If the beta is greater than one, it is more volatile than the market; if the beta is less than one, it is less volatile.

Bid: The price at which a dealer is willing to buy.

BIS: Bank for International Settlements. Based in Basel, Switzerland, it was founded in 1930 and now acts as a nonpolitical central bank for central banks. Web site: www.bis.org.

Black-Scholes Model: An option-pricing model initially derived by Fischer Black and Myron Scholes in 1973 for securities options and later refined by Black in 1976 for options on futures.

Blank: A blank disc of metal with milled edges used to make a coin.

Brazilian Mercantile and Futures Exchange: The BM&F was incorporated in July 1985. Web site: www.bmf.com.br.

Breakout/Breakaway Gap: In technical analysis, this occurs when prices break out of their trading range, leaving a gap in the chart. It is associated with an increase in volume and is regarded as a strong trend signal.

Britannia: British gold coin first issued in 1987 with a fineness of 916.6.

Broker: An intermediary between traders for physical, futures, and over-the-counter deals. Brokers receive a fixed commission predetermined between the broker and his or her client.

Budapest Stock Exchange: The Budapest Stock Exchange had its origins in the Hungarian Stock Exchange, which was formed in 1864. Following World War II, the exchange was dissolved by the government and was reestablished on June 21, 1990. Commodity trading was introduced on November 2, 2005. Web site: www.bse.hu.

Bull: Someone who expects prices to rise.

Bull Call Spread: The purchase and sale of call options at different exercise prices but with the same expiry date. The purchased (or long) calls have a lower price than the written (or short) calls. The investor expects a rise in the price of the underlying asset.

Bull Market: A market in which the trend is for prices to increase.

Bull Put Spread: The purchase and sale of put options at different exercise prices but with the same expiry date. The puts purchased have a lower exercise price than the puts written. The investor expects the price of the underlying asset to rise.

Bullion: The generic word for gold and silver in bar or ingot form. Originally meant "mint" or "melting place" from the old French word *bouillon*, which means boiling.

Bullion and Precious Metal Coins: Contemporary precious metal coins minted in unlimited numbers for investment purposes.

Butterfly Spread: The simultaneous purchase of an out-of-the-money strangle and sale of an at-the-money straddle. The buyer profits if the underlying remains stable and has limited risk in the event of a large move in either direction.

Buy Signal: In technical analysis, a chart pattern that indicates a key reversal upwards in price and the time to buy.

Calendar Spread: The simultaneous purchase and sale (or vice versa) of an option of the same strike for different months.

Call Option: An option that gives the purchaser the right, but not the obligation, to buy an asset at a predetermined price on or by a set date.

Cap: An options contract whereby the seller agrees to pay to the purchaser, in return for a premium, the difference between a reference rate and an agreed strike price when the reference exceeds the strike on or before a specific date.

Carat: Derived from the word for "carob" in various languages, it was originally equivalent to the weight of the seed of the carob tree. It has two meanings in modern usage: (1) a measure of the weight of precious stones: one carat = 0.2053 grams; (2) a measure of the proportion of gold in a gold alloy, on the basis that 24 carat is pure gold, often expressed as K or k, e.g., 18k is 75 percent gold.

Cash and Carry: The purchase (or sale) of an underlying spot asset and the simultaneous sale (or purchase) of a futures or forward contract.

CFTC: Commodity Futures Trading Commission. The U.S. government's regulatory agency for all U.S. future markets. Web site: www.cftc.gov.

Chartist: An analyst who forecasts future price trends by the technical interpretation of chart patterns based on historical prices.

Chervonetz: A Russian bullion coin, 900 fine with fine gold content of 0.2489 troy ounces and a face value of 10 rubles, which was issued in the 1970s.

Chinese Gold and Silver Exchange Society: Hong Kong's exchange first opened in 1910 and became the Chinese Gold and Silver Exchange Society in 1918. Web site: www.cgse.com.hk.

Chinese Wall: A barrier to the flow of information between two different parts of a firm's business.

Chop: Assay mark of Chinese origin. The term is now widely applied to a manufacturer's mark on bullion bars.

CIF: Cost, insurance, and freight. A CIF price includes the cost of material together with transport and insurance costs to the final specified destination.

CME Group: The CME Group was formed by the 2007 merger of the Chicago Mercantile Exchange (CME) and the Chicago Board of Trade (CBOT). Web site: www.cmegroup.com.

Coin Gold: A gold alloy, usually with a minimum fine gold content of 900, prepared for making coins, usually with silver or copper, to improve durability.

Collar: A supply contract between a buyer and a seller of a commodity, whereby the buyer is assured that he or she will not have to pay more than some maximum price, and whereby the seller is assured of receiving some minimum price.

COMEX: The Commodity Exchange in New York, a division of NYMEX.

Compound Options: These are options on options. The underlying asset is an option rather than a tangible commodity or security.

Consignment Stocks: These are gold or silver bars that are placed by an organization with a client against a guarantee of payment at the prevailing price as the metal is taken out of the stock.

Contango: The market situation where the price for future (forward) delivery is greater than the spot price.

Cost of Carry: The cost of holding a physical commodity over a period of time. The main elements are funding costs, storage, and insurance.

Covered Option: A *covered call option* is one where the writer owns the underlying asset on which the option is written. A *covered put option* is one where the writer sells the option while holding cash.

Day Order: An order to buy or sell at a particular price level, which is only valid for one business day.

Deferred Settlement: An arrangement whereby settlement of both sides of a bullion deal, metal and money, are deferred on a day-to-day basis.

Delivery: The actual transfer of the ownership of precious metal. It may not involve physical movement of metal and is usually made by a simple paper transfer in the clearing system.

Delivery Date: The specified day on which precious metal must be delivered to fulfill a contract.

Delta: Option risk parameter that measures the sensitivity of an option price to changes in the price of its underlying instrument.

Delta Hedging: A strategy undertaken by granters of options to protect their exposure. A delta hedge calculation takes into account changes in the spot price, the time to expiry, and the difference between the strike and spot prices.

Derivative: A financial instrument derived from a cash market commodity, futures contract, or other financial instrument. Derivatives can be traded on regulated exchange markets or over the counter. For example, metal futures contracts are derivatives of physical commodities; options on futures are derivatives of futures contracts.

Doré: An unrefined alloy of gold with variable quantities of silver and smaller quantities of base metals, which is produced at a mine before passing on to a refinery for upgrading to London Good Delivery standard.

Double Bottom/Double Top: In technical analysis, a double bottom occurs when the price falls to the same level twice and fails to penetrate. This signals good support. A double top is the opposite, i.e., when a price rises to the same level twice and fails to break above it, and therefore produces a level of good resistance.

Double Eagle: Gold coin with a face value of $20 issued as legal tender in the United States during the period from 1850 to 1932. It is 900 fine with a fine gold content of 0.9675 troy ounces.

Dow Theory: Developed by Charles Dow and referred to as the "six tenets of Dow Theory," it addresses market psychology and price action, and it marks the foundations of technical analysis. The six tenets are: (1) The averages discount everything. (2) There are three trends. (3) Major trends have three phases. (4) The averages must confirm each other. (5) Volume must confirm the trend. (6) A trend is assumed to be in effect until it gives definitive signals that it has reversed.

Dubai Gold and Commodities Exchange: The DGCX commenced trading in 2005. Web site: www.dgcx.ae.

Eagle: The earliest legal tender U.S. gold coin first minted in 1795. It is 900 fine.

EFP: Exchange for Physical. Actual exchange between an OTC contract and a futures contract that takes place off exchange between parties.

Elliott Wave Theory: Developed by R. N. Elliott, the approach defines markets as moving in a predetermined number of waves. Markets move in a sequence of five waves in the direction of the underlying trend and correct in a sequence of three waves. The trend movement or impulse is labeled 1–2–3–4–5 and a correction is labeled A-B-C.

ETC/ETF: Exchange-Traded Commodities (or Exchange-Traded Funds) are open-ended, listed securities that are arbitrageable with the underlying markets. ETCs trade on stock exchanges and have multiple market makers. ETCs are either backed by the physical commodity where possible (e.g., gold, silver, platinum, palladium) or are priced off commodity futures markets, thereby providing retail and institutional equity investors with the opportunity to gain exposure to major commodities through existing equity accounts.

European-Style Option: An option that can only be exercised on the expiry date.

Exchange-Traded Options: Options on futures contracts offered by a recognized futures exchange, such as NYMEX.

Exercise: The exercise by an option holder of his or her right to buy (call) or sell (put) an asset at the agreed strike price.

Exotic Options: The generic term for the more sophisticated option strategies that have features over and above basic option contracts.

Expiry Date: The last date on which an option can be exercised.

FAS 133: *See* Financial Accounting Standards Board Statement 133.

FCM: Futures Commission Merchant. The legal term for a U.S. commodity brokerage house handling futures exchange business.

Fibonacci Numbers: The Fibonacci sequence is calculated by adding any number in the series to the previous number: (1, 2, 3, 5, 8, 13, 21, 34, 55, 89, . . .). The ratio of any number in the series to the next is 0.618 and to the number two positions away, 0.382. The midpoint between 0.382 and 0.618 is 0.50. These ratios (usually shown as percentages) are known as the *Fibonacci ratios* and are used in technical analysis to calculate retracement levels during a correction. The inverse of 0.618 (1.618) is used in calculating (Elliott Wave) projections. Fibonacci ratios form an integral part of Elliott Wave Theory.

Financial Accounting Standards Board (FASB): The private sector organization responsible for establishing standards of accounting and financial reporting in the United States.

Glossary of Terms

Financial Accounting Standards Board Statement 133 (FAS 133): FAS 133 obliges U.S. companies to put all financial derivative instruments that are not used to hedge exposure on the balance sheet at market value. Companies therefore disclose unrealized gains and losses on derivatives, rather than accounting for them only at maturity.

Fineness: The proportion of precious metal in an alloy expressed as parts in 1,000.

Fine Weight: The weight of gold contained in a bar, coin, or bullion as determined by multiplying the gross weight by the fineness.

Fire Assay: A method of determining the content of a metal (most commonly gold) in an alloy involving the removal of other metals by what is in effect a combination of fire refining (for the removal of base metals) and chemical refining (for the removal of silver) and then determining the gold content by comparing the initial and final weights of the sample. Fire assay can determine the gold content of Good Delivery–type alloys to an accuracy of better than 1 part in 10,000. Fire assay is also known as *cupellation* or *gravimetric analysis*.

Flag: In technical analysis, one of the basic chart patterns. In a bull market a flag occurs when prices consolidate for a period, then continue to rise. In a bear market the converse occurs, i.e., prices resume falling after a period of consolidation.

Flat Rate Forwards: Forward contracts offering a constant contango throughout the life of the contract.

Floor: A supply contract between a buyer and seller of a commodity, whereby the seller is assured that he or she will receive at least some minimum price. This type of contract is analogous to a put option, which gives the holder the right to sell the underlying at a predetermined price.

FOB: Free on Board. An FOB price usually includes cost of transport, insurance, and loading onto a vessel at the port of departure.

Fool's Gold: Pyrites of iron sulphide, which is gold-like in appearance and can delude amateur prospectors.

Forward Premium: The difference between spot and forward quotations that will be determined by money and precious metal interest rates and storage charges.

Forward Transaction: Purchase or sale for delivery and payment at an agreed date in the future.

FSA: Financial Services Authority. The single financial services regulator in the United Kingdom. Web site: www.fsa.gov.uk.

FSMA: The Financial Services and Markets Act 2000 is the legislation that set up the Financial Services Authority and defines its powers. It came into force in late 2001.

Fundamental Analysis: The study of basic underlying factors that will affect the supply and demand of a traded commodity.

Futures Contract: An agreement made on an organized exchange to buy or sell a specific commodity or financial instrument on a set date in the future at a set price. In practice, most futures positions are "squared off" before maturity with delivery, if it takes place, in the form of a warehouse receipt.

Gamma: The sensitivity of an option's delta to changes in the price of the underlying instrument.

Gearing: The potential to magnify profits or losses by incurring exposure to large positions from an initially small investment outlay. Also known as *Leverage*.

GOFO: Gold Forward Offered Rate. The gold equivalent to the LIBOR. The rates at which dealers will lend gold on swap against U.S. dollars.

GOFRA: Gold Forward Rate Agreement. An "off balance sheet" instrument used to minimize forward gold interest rate exposure. It

Glossary of Terms

hedges the combined effect of moves in both U.S. dollar and gold interest rates with settlement in dollars.

Gold: Latin name Aurum. Chemical symbol Au. Its specific gravity is 19.32, and its melting point is 1,063 degrees centigrade.

Gold Accumulation Plans (GAPs):   Gold investment accounts whereby the investor agrees to invest a certain sum of currency in gold each month. Gold accumulated in the account can later be sold back or withdrawn as physical metal in a variety of forms, including bars, coins, or jewelry.

Gold Fixing: Held twice each working day at 10:30 a.m. and 3:00 p.m. in the City of London.

Gold FRA: Gold Lease Forward Rate Agreement. Similar to a GOFRA, but it is restricted solely to gold interest rates hedging with settlement in gold. A hedging product that is popular with those who have gold borrowing or deposit requirements. Gold FRAs are generally settled against the benchmark of U.S. dollar LIBOR minus the GOFO mean on the observation date.

Gold Loan: The provision of finance in gold for a gold-related project or business, typically in mining or jewelry inventory finance, which provides a combination of generally inexpensive funding together with built-in hedging.

Gold Parity: Legally fixed quantity of gold to which a monetary unit is pegged.

Gold Pool: The gold pool was an alliance between the central banks of Britain, Belgium, France, Italy, the Netherlands, Switzerland, the United States, and West Germany from 1961 to 1968 that endeavored to maintain the gold price at $35 per troy ounce.

Gold/Silver Ratio: The number of ounces of silver that can be bought with one ounce of gold.

Gold Standard: A monetary system with a fixed price for gold, and with gold coin either forming the whole circulation of currency within a country or with notes representing and redeemable in gold.

Gold Warrant: (1) A warrant giving the buyer the right to buy gold at a specific price on a specified value date, for which the buyer pays a premium. While similar in structure to options, warrants are securitized instruments. (2) A certificate often issued by exchanges indicating ownership of physical metal.

Good Delivery: The specification that a gold or silver bar or a platinum or palladium ingot or plate must meet in order to be acceptable for delivery in a particular terminal market or futures exchange.

Grain: One of the earliest units of weight for gold, one grain being the equivalent of one grain of wheat taken from the middle of the ear: 1 grain = 0.0648 grams or 0.002083 troy ounces; 15.43 grains = 1 gram; 480.6 grains = 1 troy ounce; 24 grains = one pennyweight. (*See also* Granules.)

Granules: Bullion, including its various alloys presented for sale in granulated form, often referred to as *grain*.

Guinea: British gold coin with a nominal value of one pound first issued in 1663 and named after gold from Guinea in West Africa. It was unofficially revalued at 21 shillings at The Great Recoinage of 1696, a value confirmed in 1717. It has a fineness of 916.6 and a fine gold content of approximately one-quarter of a troy ounce.

Hallmark: A mark or number of marks made on gold, silver, or platinum jewelry and other fabricated products to confirm that the quality is of the fineness marked on the item. See Web site: www.thegoldsmiths.co.uk.

Head and Shoulders: A three-peak pattern resembling the head and shoulders outline of a person, which is used to chart stock and commodity price trends. The pattern indicates the reversal of a trend. As prices move down to the right shoulder, a head and shoulders top is formed, meaning that prices should be falling. A reverse head and shoulders pattern has the head formation at the bottom of the chart and means that prices should be rising.

Hedge: A transaction entered into in order to offset the impact of adverse price movements of an asset.

Historic Volatility: Mathematically derived from price fluctuations of the underlying asset over a past specified period of time.

IBMA: International Bullion Master Agreement, issued by the LBMA in 1994.

IFEMA: International Foreign Exchange Master Agreement.

IMF: The International Monetary Fund was conceived at the Bretton Woods Conference in 1944 to promote international monetary cooperation and stability. It opened in Washington, D.C., in 1947. Web site: www.imf.org.

Implied Volatility: Volatility as calculated by determining the variable in the Black-Scholes option price formula from market option prices. The element of the formula that identifies the degree of supply and demand for options.

IMRO: The U.K. Investment Management Regulatory Organisation (an SRO), superseded by the Financial Services Authority in 2001.

In the Money: Refers to options with intrinsic value. For example, calls where the strike price is less than the underlying asset price or puts where the strike price is greater than the underlying asset price.

Intrinsic Value: Refers to options. The difference between the current spot price and the option strike (or exercise) price, i.e., the in-the-money element.

Iridium: Chemical symbol Ir. Its specific gravity is 22.50, and its melting point is 1,539 degrees centigrade.

ISDA: The International Swaps & Derivatives Association. Web site: www.isda.org.

ISDA Bullion Definitions: An addendum to the ISDA Master Agreement developed in 1997 by the ISDA and the LBMA to cover bullion terms. The 2005 ISDA Commodity Definitions incorporates the 1997 ISDA Bullion Definitions with some revisions.

ISDA Master Agreement: The International Swaps and Derivatives Association (ISDA) over-the-counter derivatives master agreement was drawn up by the New York–based trade association in 1987, revised in 1992, and again updated in 2002.

Islands: In technical analysis, an island top is formed when a market gaps up and then gaps down during an uptrend to leave an isolated trading session. An island bottom is found at the base of a downtrend. Islands are regarded as reversal patterns.

Istanbul Gold Exchange: The Istanbul Gold Exchange was founded in 1995. Web site: www.iab.gov.tr.

Jakarta Futures Exchange (Pt. Bursa Berjangka Jakarta): The JFX was established in August 1999. Web site: www.bbj-jfx.com.

Japanese Candlestick Theory: The principles were developed in Japan during the seventeenth century by Munehisa Homma, a rice broker. Similarly to a bar chart, a candle chart uses the open, high, low, and closing prices; however, in a candle chart a body is created between the opening and closing prices. The bodies are presented in different colors to highlight the session's direction, usually a white body for an up day (open above the close) and a black body for a down session (close below the open). Regarded as good short-term signals.

Kam: Chinese for gold.

Key Reversal: In technical analysis, a crucial change in price direction, signaling an end to either a bull or bear market.

Kilo Bar: A popular small gold bar. A one-kilogram bar 995 fine = 31.990 troy ounces, and a one-kilogram bar 999.9 fine = 32.148 troy ounces.

Knock-In: In options, an exotic option in which the option becomes valid only when a predetermined price level (usually different to the strike price) is touched during the lifetime of the option.

Knock-Out: An exotic option that is automatically terminated or "knocked out" if the price of the underlying asset reaches a predetermined level (usually different to the strike price) during the lifetime of the option.

Koala: Australian platinum coin with a fineness of 999.5.

Krugerrand: South African gold coin first issued in 1967 with a fineness of 916.6.

Lakh (or Lac): Indian term for 100,000. Frequently used to describe silver or gold orders.

LBMA: The London Bullion Market Association was formally incorporated on December 14, 1987, to represent the interests of the participants in the wholesale bullion market and to encourage the development of the London market. Web site: www.lbma.org.uk.

LBMA Good Delivery List: List of acceptable refiners of gold and silver whose bars meet the required standard (of fineness, weight, marks, and appearance) of the London Bullion Market Association.

Leverage: *See* Gearing.

Limit Order: An order that has restrictions placed on it. The customer specifies a price and the order can be executed only if the market moves to or betters that price.

Liquidity: The market tradability of an asset. A highly liquid market has a large number of buyers and sellers, or lenders, making it easy to enter or exit.

Loco: The place—location—at which a commodity, e.g., loco London gold, is physically held.

Long: A *long position* means the purchase and retention of an asset.

Long Straddle: The purchase of call and put options with the same exercise price and expiry date. The investor expects a significant increase in volatility; direction of prices is not of prime importance.

Lookback Option: A history-dependent option where the settlement at maturity is reliant not only on whether the option is in the money at expiry, but also on the maximum or minimum price achieved by the underlying asset during at least some part of the option life.

LOT: Commonly used word for a standard futures contract.

LPPM: The London Platinum and Palladium Market was formalized by a Deed of Establishment in 1987 and represents the interests of the participants in the wholesale platinum and palladium markets and encourages the development of the London and Zurich markets. Web site: www.lppm.co.uk.

LPPM Good Delivery Lists: Lists of acceptable refiners of platinum and palladium whose plates and ingots meet the required standards (of fineness, weight, marks, and appearance) of the London Platinum and Palladium Market.

MACD (Moving Convergence/Divergence Momentum Indicator): Usually the difference between the 26-day and 12-day exponential moving averages, although these parameters can be altered. A positive MACD indicates the 12-day average is above the 26-day average and highlights a positive period and/or trend. The opposite holds true for a negative reading and a downtrend.

Maple Leaf: Canadian gold coin with a fineness of 999.9 or platinum coin with a fineness of 999.5.

Glossary of Terms

Margin: Deposit, or collateral, required as security against open positions in futures, forwards, or options markets. Also called *initial margin* or *original margin*.

Margin Call: The request for additional funds to cover losses on forward or futures contracts where the price has moved against a client. *See also* Variation Margin.

Market Order: An order given to a dealer for immediate execution, to buy or sell at the best prevailing price. Also known as *at best* or *at market*.

Mark to Market: The revaluation of a position at current market price levels.

MCX: Multi-Commodity Exchange of India Ltd. Headquartered in Mumbai, MCX is a demutualized multicommodity futures exchange. The exchange began operations in November 2003. Web site: www.mcxindia.com.

Min/Max (Minimum/Maximum): A zero cost collar-style hedging strategy whereby a client sells one option in exchange for another. In bullion markets, primarily used by producers who grant call options in exchange for put options; in this case, the structure guarantees that the client will receive a minimum predetermined price in exchange for a possible opportunity loss if the actual price at maturity is above a maximum level, as determined by the strike price of the call option granted.

Moving Average: In technical analysis, this is a key trend line that is plotted on a bar chart, reflecting the progress of prices over a given period of time. (*See also* Weighted Moving Average.)

Naked Option: The sale of an option by a party who does not hold the underlying asset to back it. *See also* Covered Option.

Napoleon: French gold coin with a face value of 20 francs, bearing a portrait of Napoleon I or Napoleon III. It had a fineness of 900 and a fine gold content of 0.1867 troy ounces.

NCDEX: National Commodity and Derivatives Exchange. An online multicommodity exchange located in Mumbai, it began operations in December 2003. Web site: www.ncdex.com.

Noble: Isle of Man platinum coin with a fineness of 999.5.

Numismatics: The specialized sector of the coin business for the study and collection of rare coins and other media of exchange, particularly those with archaeological and historic interest.

NYMEX: A U.S. futures exchange consisting of two divisions, NYMEX (the New York Mercantile Exchange) and COMEX (the Commodities Exchange). Web site: www.nymex.com.

Offer: The price at which a dealer is willing to sell.

Open Interest: On a futures exchange, the daily statistic that indicates the number of open contracts, i.e., those that have not been fulfilled or closed out.

Open Outcry: A style of trading conducted on a futures exchange in a ring or a pit where dealers face each other, calling out the price, contract, month, and number of contracts.

Open Position: A market position that has not been closed out.

Option: An option is the right, but not the obligation, to buy and sell a predetermined quantity of an underlying asset at a predetermined price by or on a defined date.

Ore: Originally from the Old English for crude or unwrought metal. It refers to any economic mineral deposit of precious or other metals.

Osmium: Chemical symbol Os. Its specific gravity is 22.50, and its melting point is 2,700 degrees centigrade.

OTC: Over the Counter. Transactions that are quoted and conducted between parties on a principal-to-principal basis as opposed to being traded via a broker on an exchange.

Glossary of Terms

OTC Option: Over-the-counter options are not traded on recognized future exchanges but between organizations acting as principals, or between a bank and its client.

Out of the Money: Refers to options with only time value (i.e., no intrinsic value); e.g., calls where the strike price is greater than the underlying asset price or puts where the strike price is less than the underlying price.

Overbought: A market in which the price, under excessive buying pressure, has risen too high and too fast without genuine fundamental support to maintain the new level.

Oversold: A market that has fallen too far and too fast under excessive selling pressure and is expected to move back to a higher, more neutral level.

Palladium: A metallic element, chemical symbol Pd. Its specific gravity is 12.00, and its melting point is 1,555 degrees centigrade.

Palladium Fixing: Held twice each working day at 9:45 a.m. and 2:00 p.m. in the City of London.

Panda: Chinese gold coin of 999.9 quality, first made in 1982.

Panning: The classic and simple method of mining alluvial gold.

Paper Gold: A term used to describe gold contracts such as loco London deals and futures contracts that do not necessarily involve the delivery of physical gold.

Pennyweight: Originally the weight of a silver penny in Britain in the Middle Ages, which is still widely used in North America as the unit of weight in the jewelry trade: 20 pennyweights = 1 troy ounce.

Philharmoniker: Austrian gold coin of 999.9 fineness, first issued in 1989.

PIA: The Personal Investment Authority took over from LAUTRO and FIMBRA in 1994 as an SRO for most firms conducting investment business with the private investor. It was superseded by the FSA in 2001 when the FSMA came into force.

Platinum: Chemical symbol Pt. Its specific gravity is 21.45, and its melting point is 1,773 degrees centigrade.

Platinum Fixing: Held twice each working day at 9:45 a.m. and 2:00 p.m. in the City of London.

Platinum Group Metals: Platinum, palladium, iridium, osmium, rhodium, and ruthenium.

Precious Metals: Metals of great value being gold, silver, platinum, palladium, and other platinum group metals.

Put Option: A contract that gives the buyer the right, but not the obligation, to sell a specified amount of an asset at a predetermined price on or before a specified date.

Put Spread: An options position composed of the purchase of a put option at one level and the sale of a put option at some lower level. The premium received by selling one option reduces the cost of buying the other, but participation is limited if the underlying goes down.

Quartation: The process in which silver is separated from gold by dissolving it out with nitric acid, more commonly referred to as *nitric acid parting*.

Refining: The separating and purifying of precious metals from other metals.

Resistance: In technical analysis, the price level where selling is expected to emerge.

Rho: A measure of an option's sensitivity to a change in interest rates; this will impact both the future price of the option and the time value of the premium. Its impact increases with the maturity of the option.

Rhodium: Chemical symbol Rh. Its specific gravity is 12.44, and its melting point is 1,966 degrees centigrade.

Risk: The exposure to adverse market movements, mischance, or the possibility of losing money.

Rolled Gold: The process in which a layer of carat gold alloy is mechanically bonded to another metal.

RSI (Relative Strength Index):   Developed by J. Welles Wilder, the RSI compares the magnitude of an instrument's gains to its losses over a set period (usually 14 days). This is a momentum oscillator and provides information such as overbought or oversold conditions and divergence between price and indicator.

Ruthenium: Chemical symbol Ru. Its specific gravity is 12.20, and its melting point is 2,500 degrees centigrade.

Scrap Gold: The broad term for any gold that is sent back to a refiner or processor for recycling.

Sell Signal: In technical analysis, a chart pattern that indicates a key reversal downwards in price.

Settlement Date: The date on which a contract must be fully paid for and delivered. It is the general practice in international precious metals markets for settlement to take place two business days after the transaction date, i.e., spot.

Settlement Price: In futures markets, the price that is set by the exchange committee at the end of each trading day and that is used by the clearinghouse to market open positions and assess margin calls.

Settlement Risk: The risk that arises when payments are not exchanged simultaneously, generally arising because of time differences. One party to a transaction must effect payment or delivery in an earlier time zone without having confirmation of the receipt of a reciprocal asset in a later time zone.

SFA: The Securities and Futures Authority (an SRO) was responsible for the regulation of investment business in the United Kingdom. It was superseded by the FSA in 2001 when the FSMA came into force.

Shanghai Futures Exchange: The Shanghai Futures Exchange was formed in December 1999. Web site: www.shfe.com.

Shanghai Gold Exchange: The Shanghai Gold Exchange was founded in 2002. Web site: www.sge.sh.

Short: A *short position* means the sale of an asset not yet owned.

Short Straddle: The sale of a call and put option with the same exercise price and expiry date. The investor has a neutral view of the underlying asset and expects limited price fluctuation.

Silver: Latin name Argentum. Its chemical symbol is Ag, its specific gravity is 10.49, and its melting point is 960 degrees centigrade.

Silver Fixing: Held each working day at 12:00 p.m. in the City of London.

Singapore Exchange Limited (SGX):   The Singapore Exchange was inaugurated on December 1, 1999, following the merger of the Stock Exchange of Singapore (SES) and the Singapore International Monetary Exchange (SIMEX). Web site: www.sgx.com.

Smelting: The process of melting ores or concentrates to separate out the metal content from impurities.

Souk: The local name for *market* used throughout the Arab world.

Sovereign: British gold coin with face value of one pound sterling, a fineness of 916.6, and a fine gold content of 0.2354 troy ounces.

Glossary of Terms

Spot Deferred: Hybrid forward contract offering floating interest rates and no fixed delivery. It is more flexible than conventional spot or forward contracts.

Spot Settlement: Delivery of metal and payment of money, which takes place two business days after the transaction date.

SROs: Self Regulatory Organizations were established under the Financial Services Act of 1986 to carry out the regulation of most institutions involved in investment activities in the United Kingdom. Under the FSMA, the role played by the SROs was taken over by the FSA in 2001.

Standard Bar/Plate/Ingot: Refers to any of the following: (1) Gold bar weighing approximately 400 ounces or 12.5 kilograms and having a minimum fineness of 995 parts per 1,000 pure gold. (2) Silver bar weighing approximately 1,000 ounces with a minimum fineness of 999. (3) Platinum or palladium plate or ingot between 1 and 6 kilograms with a minimum fineness of 999.5.

Standard Deviation: Statistical measure of the degree to which an individual value in a probability distribution tends to vary from the mean of the distribution. Indicates probability of a variable or price falling within a certain width or band around the mean.

Stochastics: Developed by George Lane, this momentum oscillator shows the location of the current close relative to the high/low range over a specified period. Closing levels near the top of the range indicate buying pressure, while closing levels near the base of the range indicate selling pressure.

Stop Loss: An order placed to liquidate an open position when the price reaches a specified level in order to prevent further losses. These orders are only handled on a *best efforts* basis, as there is no guarantee that an order can be executed at the specified price if the market is highly volatile and prices move so fast, or *gap*, that the order cannot be carried out at the price requested.

Straddle: Purchase or sale of call and put options for the same underlying asset with the same expiry date and strike price.

Strangle: In options, a speculative strategy of either buying or selling puts and calls, each with the same expiry date but with different strike prices.

Strike Price: In options, the predetermined price at which an option may be exercised.

Support: In technical analysis, the price level where new buyers are expected to emerge.

Swap: Refers to any of the following: (1) Simultaneous purchase and sale of spot against forward. (2) An exchange between different locations. (3) A swap or exchange of different size of quality of bullion bars or platinum and/or palladium ingots or plates. (4) An agreement whereby a floating price is exchanged for a fixed price over a specified period.

Switch: Simultaneous purchase and sale of the same asset for different maturity dates.

Tael: Traditional Chinese unit of weight for gold: one tael = 1.20337 troy ounces = 37.4290 grams. The nominal fineness of a Hong Kong tael bar is 990, but in Taiwan 5- and 10-tael bars can be 999.9 fine.

Technical Analysis: The study of historical prices, examining patterns of price changes, rates of change, and changes in volume of trading and open interest, in order to predict future price behavior. Technical analysis is usually performed in chart or graph form.

Theta: In options, the rate of change in the value of the option with respect to time with all else remaining the same.

Time Value: Refers to options. The difference between an option's market price and its intrinsic value.

Tokyo Commodities Exchange: TOCOM was established on November 1, 1984, as a merger of the Tokyo Textile Exchange, the Tokyo Rubber Exchange, and the Tokyo Gold Exchange. Web site: www.tocom.or.jp.

Tola: Traditional Indian unit of weight for gold: One tola = 0.375 troy ounces = 11.6638 grams. The most popular sized bar is 10 tola = 3.75 troy ounces. Weights are for 999.9 gold purity.

Tom/Next: Refers to the time period commencing one business day forward from the present and ending one business day later (usually spot). In precious metals, generally refers to the swap rate for borrowing or lending metal versus U.S. dollars for this time period, which is typically used to manage short-term liquidity flows.

Trend/Trend Line: In technical analysis, *trend* is defined as a directional move over a period of time. There are three types: up, down, and sideways. A *trend line* is a straight line that connects two or more price points, extending it into the future to act as a support or resistance. Trend lines are important in that they identify and confirm trends. (*See also* Support and Resistance.)

Troy Ounce: The traditional unit of weight used for precious metals, which was attributed to a weight used in Troyes, France, in medieval times: one troy ounce is equal to 1.0971428 ounces avoirdupois.

Unallocated Account: An account where specific bars are not set aside and the customer has a general entitlement to the metal. This is the most convenient, cheapest, and most commonly used method of holding metal. The holder is an unsecured creditor.

Underlying: The variable on which a futures, option, or other derivative contract is based.

Value Date: The date agreed between parties for the settlement of a transaction.

Vanilla Option: A standard transaction that is not tailored to the needs of either party. A plain vanilla option pays out the difference between the strike price of the option and the spot price of the underlying at the time of the exercise.

Variation Margin: Additional margin, or collateral, payable by an investor, resulting from an adverse movement in the price of the underlying asset in a forward, futures, or options contract.

Vega: A measure of how much an option's price will change as the volatility of the underlying fluctuates.

Volatility: Refers to options. The rate of change in the price of the underlying asset. (*See also* Implied Volatility and Historic Volatility.)

Volume: On futures exchanges, the number of contracts traded in a session.

Vreneli: Swiss gold coin with a face value of 20 francs issued as legal tender in the period from 1897 to 1935. It had a fineness of 900 and a fine gold content of 0.1867 troy ounces.

Wafer: Small, thin gold bars popular in the Middle East, South East Asia, and Japan.

Warehouse Receipt: A warehouse or depository receipt is issued when delivery is taken on a futures exchange. It specifies the quantity and fineness of the precious metal held.

Weighted Moving Average: Used in technical analysis, a weighted moving average gives a greater weighting to more recent price data, as opposed to a *simple moving average* that gives equal weighting to all prices. (*See also* Moving Average.)

White Gold: A gold alloy containing whitening agents such as silver, palladium, or nickel as well as other base metals; often used as a setting for diamond jewelry.

Writer: In options, the seller or granter of the option.

Yield Curve: The relationship between interest rate yields and maturity lengths. The yield curve normally has a positive slope (i.e., upwards) because yields on long-term interest rates usually exceed short-term yields. An investor expects a higher return for holding an asset for a longer time; hence yields normally increase with maturity length.

Zero-Cost Option: An option strategy under which one option is purchased by simultaneously selling another option of equal value. (*See also* Min/Max.)

Properties of Gold

(Courtesy of the World Gold Council: www.gold.org.)

 Gold (symbol Au) has an atomic number of 79, i.e., each gold atom has 79 protons in its nucleus. The atomic mass of the gold atom is 196.967, and the atomic radius is 0.1442 nanometers. Interestingly this is smaller than would be predicted by theory.

The arrangement of outer electrons around the gold nucleus is related to gold's characteristic yellow color. The color of a metal is based on transitions of electrons between energy bands. The conditions for the intense absorption of light at the wavelengths necessary to produce the typical gold color are fulfilled by a transition from the d band to unoccupied positions in the conduction band. Gold's attractive warm color has led to its widespread use in decoration.

While the number of protons in a gold nucleus is fixed at 79, the number of neutrons can vary from one atom to another, giving a number of isotopes of gold. However, there is only one stable nonradioactive isotope accounting for all naturally found gold.

The crystal structure for metallic gold is face-centered cubic (FCC). See Figure D-1.

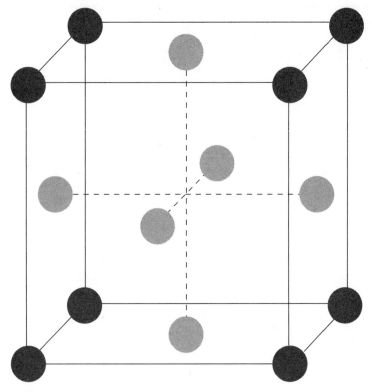

Figure D-1
The Crystal Structure of Metallic Gold

This crystal structure contributes to gold's very high ductility since FCC lattices are particularly suitable for allowing the movement of dislocations in the lattice. Such dislocation movement is essential for achieving high ductility.

The density of gold (19.3 grams per cubic centimeter) depends on both its atomic mass and the crystal structure. This makes gold rather heavy compared to some other common materials. For example, aluminum has a density of 2.7 grams per cubic centimeter, and even steel's density is only 7.87 grams per cubic centimeter.

Properties of Gold

The melting point of pure gold is 1,064 degrees centigrade, although when alloyed with other elements such as silver or copper, the gold alloy will melt over a range of temperatures. The boiling point of gold, when gold transforms from the liquid to gaseous state, is 2,860 degrees centigrade.

The ability of gold to efficiently transfer heat and electricity is bettered only by copper and silver, but unlike these metals, gold does not tarnish, making it indispensable in electronics.

The electrical resistivity of gold is 0.022 micro-ohm per meter at 20 degrees centigrade. The thermal conductivity is 310 watts per meter per kelvin at the same temperature. The corrosion resistance of gold is perhaps one of its most useful properties. Electrode potentials are a useful method for representing the tendency of a metal to corrode. Electrode potentials are measured with reference to hydrogen, and an electrochemical series can be prepared for metals as indicated in Table D-1. Not surprisingly, gold is at the top of the series, indicating its high corrosion resistance. In practice, it is corroded only by a mixture of nitric and hydrochloric acid (aqua regia). In everyday use gold does not tarnish.

Table D-1
Electrode Potentials for Various Metals

ELECTRODE POTENTIAL (VOLTS)	ELEMENT
11.5	Gold
10.8	Silver
20.4	Iron
20.8	Zinc
21.66	Aluminum

The metal gold is extremely malleable (the extent to which a material can undergo deformation in compression before failure). In the annealed state, it can be hammered cold into a translucent wafer 0.000013 centimeters thick. One ounce of gold can be beaten into a sheet covering over 9 square meters and 0.000018 centimeters thick.

Gold is also ductile (degree of extension that takes place before failure of a material in tension), and one ounce can be drawn into 80 kilometers (50 miles) of thin gold wire (5 microns diameter) to make electrical contacts and bonding wire.

The Young's modulus of elasticity of a material is related to rigidity or stiffness and is defined as the ratio between the stress applied and the elastic strain it produces. Gold has a Young's modulus of 79 giga pascals, which is very similar to silver, but significantly lower than iron or steel.

Hardness is defined as the ability of a material to resist surface abrasion. The relative hardness of materials was historically assessed using a list of materials arranged in such order that any material in the list will scratch any one below it. Thus, diamond, the hardest substance known, heads the list with a hardness index of 10 while talc is at the bottom with a hardness index of 1. On this scale, gold has a value of 2.5 to 3, i.e., it is a soft metal. For more accurate measurements the Vickers hardness measurement (Hv) is used, and gold has a value of approximately 25 Hv in the annealed condition.

Gold demonstrates excellent biocompatibility within the human body (the main reason for its use as a dental alloy), and as a result there are a number of direct applications of gold as a medical material. Gold also possesses a high degree of resistance to bacterial colonization, and because of this it is the material of choice for implants that are at risk of infection, such as those in the inner ear.

Gold forms a number of interesting compounds based on the familiar oxidation states 11 and 13. Gold-based chemicals include halides, cyanides, and sulfides.

The basic properties of gold are listed in Table D-2.

Properties of Gold

Properties of Gold

PROPERTY	CHARACTERISTIC
Atomic weight	196.97
Atomic number	79
Number of naturally occurring isotopes	1
Melting point (degrees centigrade)	1,064
Crystal structure	FCC
Density (grams per cubic centimeter)	19.3
Thermal conductivity (watts per meter per kelvin)	310
Electrical resistivity (micro-ohm per meter at 20 degrees centigrade)	0.022
Young's modulus (giga pascals)	79
Hardness (Hv)	25
Tensile stress (mega pascal)	124
0.2 % proof stress (mega pascal)	30
Poissons ratio	0.42

Bar Weights and Their Agreed Fine Gold Content

(Courtesy of the London Bullion Market Association.)

GROSS WEIGHT	FINE GOLD CONTENT IN OUNCES TROY PER BAR		
	995.0 ASSAY	999.0 ASSAY	999.9 ASSAY
1 kilogram	31.990	32.119	32.148
0.5 kilogram	15.995	16.059	16.074
0.25 kilogram	7.998	8.030	8.037
200 grams	6.398	6.424	6.430
100 grams	3.199	3.212	3.215
50 grams	1.600	1.607	1.608
20 grams	0.640	0.643	0.643
10 grams	0.321	0.322	0.322
5 grams	0.161	0.161	0.161
100 ounces	99.500	99.900	99.990
50 ounces	49.750	49.950	49.995
25 ounces	24.875	24.975	24.998
10 ounces	9.950	9.990	9.999
5 ounces	4.975	4.995	5.000
1 ounce	0.995	0.999	1.000
10 tolas	3.731	3.746	3.750
5 taels	5.987	6.011	6.017

Index

Note: Page numbers followed by *f* refer to figures and those followed by *t* refer to tables

Accelerated supply, 41, 163
Aliquot, 163
Allocated gold, 69–70, 111–112
Allocated gold accounts, 70–71, 141–142, 158, 163
Alloys, 163
Al-Qaeda, 5
American-style options, 163
AngloGold Ashanti, 40, 150
Arbitrage, 106, 164
Argentina, 16, 30
ARM, 161
Ashanti Goldfields, 6
Asia, 116, 117, 122
    (*See also individual countries*)
Asian financial crisis (1990s), 122
Asian-style options, 164
Asia/Pacific trading operations, 65
Ask, 164
Assay, 164
Assay mark, 164
Assay office, 164
Assayers, 164
Asset Strategy funds, 18
Assets under management (AUM), 83
ASX (Australian Securities Exchange), 164
At the money, 164
AUM (assets under management), 83
Australia, 1–2, 17, 37, 38, 149

Australian dollar, 85
Australian mining industry, 66
Australian producers, 62, 82
Australian Securities Exchange (ASX), 164
Austria, 17, 29*t*, 39, 42
    Oesterreichisch Nationalbank, 42
Average strike options, 164
Averaging, 164–165
Avery, Mike, 18
Avoirdupois ounces, 69

Backwardation, 13, 59, 157, 165
Banca d'Italia, 42
Banco de España, 42
Banco de Portugal, 42
Bank for International Settlements (BIS), 130, 166
Bank of England, 43–44, 86–88, 151, 165
Bank of Greece, 42
Bank of Nova Scotia–ScotiaMocatta, 73, 87
Banks:
    clearing services of, 87
    gold accounts in, 69–71, 140–142
    lending of gold by, 119
    as market makers, 12–13
    projected collapse of, 8
    (*See also* Bullion banks; Central banks)

Index

Banque centrale du Luxembourg, 45
Banque de France, 42
Banque Nationale de Belgique, 42
Bar charts, 165
Barclays Bank PLC, 73, 74, 87
Barclays Capital Commodity Investor
    Solutions, 143
Barrick Gold, 133, 149
Barrier options, 62, 82, 165
Bars, 71
    (*See also* Gold bars)
Bear, 165
Bear call spread, 165
Bear market, 165
Bear put spread, 165–166
Belgium, 17, 29*t*, 37, 39, 42
    Banque Nationale de Belgique, 42
Benchmark, 72, 75, 155
Benchmark rates, 79–80
Bermuda-style options, 166
Bernanke, Ben, 22
Beta, 166
Bid, 166
BIS (*see* Bank for International
    Settlements)
Black-Scholes model, 166
Blanchard and Company Inc., 133
Blanks, 166
BM&F (Brazilian Mercantile and
    Futures Exchange), 166
Borrowing gold (*see* Lending and
    borrowing gold)
Brazil, 3, 27, 48
Brazilian Mercantile and Futures
    Exchange (BM&F), 166
Breakout/breakaway gap, 166
Britannia, 166
Brokers, 167
Brown, Gordon, 2, 35
Budapest Stock Exchange, 167
Bull, 167
Bull call spread, 167
Bull market, 167
Bull put spread, 167
Bullion, 167
Bullion and precious metal coins, 167
Bullion banks, 65–91
    clearing process, 86–88
    gold option market, 81–83
    hedge funds, 83–86
    liquidity, 72
    London gold fixing, 73–74
    major trading centers, 65–67

    market conventions, 90–91
    market makers, 67–68
    spot gold trading, 68–71
    trading directly with, 141
    trading gold interest rates, 76–81
    turnover, 88–90
Bundesbank, 4
Bush, George W., 5
Butterfly spread, 167
Buy signal, 167
Buying of gold, 27, 33–36
    by central banks, 2–3, 16–17, 25
    in India, 22–23
    London gold fixing, 74–75

Calendar spread, 168
California, 8
Call options, 43, 62, 82, 85, 168
Cambior Inc., 6
Canada, 17, 37
Cap, 168
Carat, 116, 168
Cash and carry, 168
Central Bank and Financial Services
    Authority of Ireland, 42
Central Bank of Russia, 26, 32, 125
Central bankers, public opinion of, 4
Central banks:
    allocated gold in, 70–71
    and conspiracy theories, 134
    and deflation, 7
    as drivers of gold price, 16–17
    gold holdings/reserves of, 25–26, 29,
        33–35, 151
    inflation and economic control by, 22
    in late 1990s, 1–2
    lending of gold by, 54, 76–78, 80–81
    operating funds for, 51
    selling of gold by, 36–38
CFTC (Commodity Futures Trading
    Commission), 168
CGSE (*see* Chinese Gold and Silver
    Exchange Society)
Chartist, 168
Chase Manhattan Corp., 131
Chervonetz, 168
China, 2–3
    as buyer of gold, 16, 30, 32
    buying gold gifts in, 117
    gold holdings/reserves of, 17, 26, 27*t*,
        28*t*, 30–31, 33–36, 34*t*
    gold jewelry consumption in, 150
    gold production in, 149

Index

gold-giving occasions in, 120
People's Bank of China (PBoC), 30
as top gold producer, 12
Chinese Gold and Silver Exchange
    Society (CGSE), 97–100, 168
Chinese wall, 169
Chop, 169
CIF (cost, insurance, and freight), 169
Citigroup Inc., 131
Clearing, 68, 86–88
Clinton, Bill, 131
CME Globex, 104, 107, 140
CME Group, 169
Coin gold, 139, 169
Collar, 169
COMEX (*see* Commodity Exchange)
Comex Gold Trust, 110
COMEX/NYMEX hedging, 72
Commodities, 9, 13
Commodity Exchange (COMEX), 66,
    104, 106–107, 130, 169
Commodity funds, 83
Commodity Futures Trading
    Commission (CFTC), 168
Compound options, 169
Consignment stocks, 118–119, 169
Conspiracy theories, 130–135,
    159–160
Consumption of gold, 150
Contango, 13, 59–62, 157, 169
Cost, insurance, and freight (CIF), 169
Cost of carry, 169
Covered option, 170
Credit Suisse, 66
Crockett, Andrew, 48
Cultural views of gold, 117–118
Currency:
    gold as, 18, 25, 130
    gold prices and, 9–12, 10*f*
    trading gold against, 85
Cyprus central bank, 43

Day orders, 170
De Nederlandsche Bank, 42
Deferred settlements, 170
Deflation, 7
Delivery, 170
Delivery date, 170
Delta, 43, 170
Delta hedging, 170
Demand for gold:
    investment demand, 12–15
    physical demand, 14–15, 115–116

Derivatives, 170
Deutsche Bank AG, 73, 87, 131
Deutsche Bundesbank, 42
DGCX (*see* Dubai Gold and
    Commodities Exchange)
Digitals, 82
Dimon, Jamie, 8
Diversification, 17–19, 125–126
Dollar (*see* Australian dollar; U.S. dollar)
Doré, 170
Double bottom/double top, 170–171
Double eagle, 171
Dow Theory, 171
Drivers of gold price, 9–24
    central banks, 16–17
    diversification, 17–19
    faith in financial system, 22–23
    inflation, 21–22
    investment demand, 12–14
    miners, 20–21
    physical demand vs. investment
        demand, 14–15
    sentiment, 19–20
    U.S. dollar, 9–12
Dubai Gold and Commodities
    Exchange (DGCX), 101–103,
    171
Duisenberg, Wim, 38

Eagle, 171
East Asia, scrap gold from, 121
EcbGA (*see* European central bank Gold
    Agreement)
EFP (*see* Exchange for Physical)
Elliott Wave Theory, 171
Equities, 138
ETFs (*see* Exchange-traded funds)
Euroland 11, 38–39
European Central Bank, 29*t,* 33, 38, 42,
    45, 125
European central bank Gold Agreement
    (EcbGA), 2, 38–51, 159
    in conspiracy theories, 132
    and IMF, 47–52
    Mark I, 39–41
    Mark I vs. Mark II, 43–44
    Mark II, 41–43
    Mark II vs. Mark III, 46–47
    Mark III, 44–45
    and selling of gold, 17
    weekly financial statement, 51–52
European central banks, 4–5
    (*See also individual banks*)

Index

European trading operations, 65

European-style options, 172

Euros, gold price and, 5–7, 5f, 6f, 86

Euro/U.S. dollar exchange rate, 9–11, 10f–11f

Exchange for Physical (EFP), 105–107, 171

Exchange rate, euro/U.S. dollar, 9–11, 10f–11f

Exchange-traded funds (ETFs), 109–114
  allocated gold accounts vs., 142
  allocated gold in, 70, 111–112
  for gold, 109–111, 111f
  investing in, 142–143
  and investment demand, 13–14
  SPDR Gold Shares, 112–114

Exercise (of options), 172

Expiry date, 172

Exposure to gold (see Investing in gold)

FAS 133, 173

FASB (Financial Accounting Standards Board), 172

FCM (Futures Commission Merchant), 172

Federal Reserve, 4

Federal Reserve Bank of New York, 142

Fibonacci numbers, 172

Financial Accounting Standards Board (FASB), 172

Financial Accounting Standards Board Statement 133 (FAS 133), 173

Financial crisis of 2007–2008, 21–22, 50

Financial health, 135

Financial Services and Markets Act 2000 (FSMA), 174

Financial Services Authority (FSA), 174

Financial system, faith in, 22–23, 129

Fine gold content, 69, 71, 199

Fine weight, 173, 199

Fineness, 173
  CGSE trades, 97–100
  cultural differences in, 116
  DGCX trades, 102
  NYMEX trades, 105

Finland, 39, 42
  Suomen Pankki, 42

Fire assay, 173

Fixing, gold (see Gold fixing)

Flags, 173

Flat rate forwards, 173

Floating interest rate, 79–80

Floor, 173

FOB (Free on Board), 173

Fool's gold, 174

Forward premium, 174

Forward price, 13, 60

Forward transaction, 174

Forwardation, 59

Forwards market making, 91

France, 17, 27t, 29t, 39, 42
  Banque de France, 42

Free on Board (FOB), 173

Freeport-McMoRan Grasberg mine, 150

Freud, Sigmund, 124

FSA (Financial Services Authority), 174

FSMA (Financial Services and Markets Act 2000), 174

Fundamental analysis, 174

Futures Commission Merchant (FCM), 172

Futures contracts, 42, 47, 139–140, 174

Gamma, 174

GAPs (gold accumulation plans), 175

Gartman, Dennis, 25

GATA, 133, 135, 160

GBS UK, 110, 111f

Gearing, 174

Germany, 4, 27t, 29t, 39, 42, 54
  Deutsche Bundesbank, 42

GFMS, 152–153

Gifts, gold, 117–118, 120–121

GLD Trust, 112, 113

GOFO (see Gold Forward Offered Rate)

GOFRA (Gold Forward Rate Agreement), 174–175

Gold, 175
  colors of, 123, 193
  correlation to other assets, 126f
  as currency, 18, 25, 130
  frequently asked questions about, 149–161
  and inflation, 4, 4f, 126, 128–129, 129f
  interest on gold in, 56–58
  marginalization of, 84
  properties of, 193–197, 194f, 195t, 197t
  as "risk" asset, 8
  scrap, 121–122, 185
  and September 11 attacks, 5
  (See also Physical gold; specific topics)

Index

Gold accounts, 69–71
  allocated, 70–71, 141–142
  unallocated, 70, 140–141
Gold accumulation plans (GAPs), 175
Gold as a Strategic Asset (Michaud,
  Michaud, and Pulvermacher), 125
Gold bars, 69, 119, 156–157, 199
Gold Bullion Securities, 110
Gold ETFs, 109–111, 111*f*, 142–143
Gold exchanges, 93–108
  Chinese Gold and Silver Exchange
    Society, 97–100
  Dubai Gold and Commodities
    Exchange, 101–103
  New York Mercantile Exchange,
    104–107
  online, 107
  Shanghai Futures Exchange, 100–101
  Tokyo Commodity Exchange,
    93–97
Gold fixing, 37, 72–75, 155, 175
Gold forward, 76–78
Gold Forward Offered Rate (GOFO),
  80, 155, 174
Gold Forward Rate Agreement
  (GOFRA), 174–175
Gold FRA (Gold Lease Forward Rate
  Agreement), 175
Gold in dollars, 57
Gold in gold, 57
Gold interest rate swaps (gold IRSs), 58,
  78–79
Gold Lease Forward Rate Agreement
  (gold FRA), 175
Gold leases, 57
Gold loan, 175
Gold market, 11
  and EcbGA Mark III, 44
  and global wealth, 15
  for gold sold before being mined, 63
  influential groups in, 158
  regulation of, 159
  size of, 68
  (*See also* Bullion banks)
Gold option market, 81–83
Gold parity, 175
Gold pool, 175
Gold reserves, 1, 27*t*, 28*t*
  of central banks, 25–26
  increase in, 17
  ownership of, 2
  and supply-and-demand trends, 12
  (*See also* Holders of gold)

Gold sheets, 123
Gold standard, 176
Gold swap rate, 78
Gold swaps, 76–78
Gold warrant, 176
Gold wire, 123
Goldman Sachs Group Inc., 131
Gold/silver ratio, 148, 148*f*, 175
Gold-trading centers, 65–67
Good delivery, 153–154, 176
Governments, conspiracy theories and,
  132–134
Grain, 176
Granules, 176
Greece, 7, 8, 42, 43
  Bank of Greece, 42
Green gold, 123
Greenspan, Alan, 130
Gueguina, Maria, 26, 125
Guinea, 176

Hallmarks, 176
Head and shoulders, 176–177
Heavily Indebted Poor Countries
  (HIPC), 47, 48
Hedge funds, 18, 83–86
Hedges, 177
Hedging, 3, 5, 20–21
  argument about, 61–62
  by producers, 40, 41, 54, 56, 58–63,
    81–83
HIPC (*see* Heavily Indebted Poor
  Countries)
Historic volatility, 177
History of gold, 124
Holders of gold, 27–33, 27*t*–29*t*
  central banks, 34*t*, 151
  countries, 27*t*–29*t*, 151
  EbcGA institutions, 42
  gold ETFs, 111
  (*See also* Gold reserves)
Hong Kong, 28*t*, 116, 126–127
HSBC Bank USA NA, 73, 87

IBMA (International Bullion Master
  Agreement), 177
"Identifiable investment" for gold, 150
IFEMA (International Foreign Exchange
  Master Agreement), 177
IMF (*see* International Monetary Fund)
Implied volatility, 177
IMRO (Investment Management
  Regulatory Organisation), 177

Index

In the money, 177
India:
  as buyer of gold, 16, 27, 30
  buying gold gifts in, 117
  citizen buyers of gold in, 22–23, 127
  gold holdings of, 27t, 28t, 33–34, 34t
  gold jewelry consumption in, 150
  gold-giving occasions in, 120
Indonesia, 28t
Industrial demand, 14
Inflation, 7
  as driver of gold price, 21–22
  price of gold relative to, 4, 4f, 126,
    128–129, 129f
Interbank option market, 85
Interest on gold, in dollars vs. gold,
  56–58
Interest rates:
  in financial crises, 7
  on gold, 53, 54, 55t, 76–81,
    154–155
International Bullion Master Agreement
  (IBMA), 177
International Foreign Exchange Master
  Agreement (IFEMA), 177
International Monetary Fund (IMF),
  27t, 30–32, 46–50, 52, 177
International Swaps & Derivatives
  Association (ISDA), 178
Intrinsic value, 177
Investing in gold, 137–145
  allocated gold accounts, 141–142
  buy-and-hold nature of, 35
  equities, 138
  exchange-traded funds, 142–143
  futures, 139–140
  physical gold, 138–139
  structured notes, 143–144
  unallocated gold accounts, 140–141
Investment demand, 12–15
Investment Management Regulatory
  Organisation (IMRO), 177
Iran, 27
Ireland, 7, 39, 42, 44
  Central Bank and Financial Services
    Authority of Ireland, 42
Iridium, 177
ISDA (International Swaps &
  Derivatives Association), 178
ISDA bullion definitions, 178
ISDA Master Agreement, 178
iShares, 110, 111f
Islands, 178

Istanbul Gold Exchange, 178
Italy, 7, 27t, 29t, 39, 42
  Banca d'Italia, 42

Jakarta Futures Exchange (Pt. Bursa
  Berjangka Jakarta), 178
Japan, 27t, 28t
Japanese candlestick theory, 178
Jewelry, 14, 115, 123
  consignment stocks, 118–119
  country consumption rates for, 150
  cultural views of, 117–118
  as greatest use of gold, 121
J.P. Morgan & Co., Ltd., 131, 133
JPMorgan Chase & Co., 8
JPMorgan Chase Bank, 87

Kam, 178
Kerry, John, 5
Key reversal, 178
Kilo bar, 179
King, Mervyn, 21–22
Knock-in, 62, 179
Knock-out, 62, 179
Koala, 179
Korea, 28t
Krugerrand, 179

Lakh (lac), 71, 179
LBMA (*see* London Bullion Market
  Association)
LBMA Good Delivery List, 179
Lease rate swaps, 58, 78–79
Leases, 42, 47, 57–58
Lending and borrowing gold, 53–63
  banks as lenders, 119
  calculating interest, 57–58
  central banks as lenders, 76–78,
    80–81
  contango, 59–62
  hedging, 58–59, 62–63
  and IMF, 50–51
  interest in dollars vs. gold, 56–58
  producers as borrowers, 54, 56
  yield curve, 54–56
  yield on gold, 53–54
LIBOR, 80
LIBOR minus GOFO, 80
LIBOR-GOFO rates, 55, 55t
Limit orders, 179
Liquidity, 72, 179
Loco, 180
Loco London, 37, 68, 99, 101, 103, 155

Index

Loco swaps, 156
London, 66, 86
London bullion market, 86
London Bullion Market Association
    (LBMA), 67, 68, 86, 153–154, 179
London Gold Bullion Securities, 110
London gold fixing, 37, 72–75, 155
London Gold Market Fixing Ltd.,
    73–75
London Good Delivery bars, 69,
    156–157
London market, 67–68
London Platinum and Palladium
    Market (LPPM), 180
London Precious Metals Clearing
    Limited (LPMCL), 87, 88
Long position, 180
Long straddle, 180
Long-Term Capital Management
    (LTCM), 132
Lookback options, 180
LOTs, 180
LPMCL (see London Precious Metals
    Clearing Limited)
LPPM (London Platinum and
    Palladium Market), 180
LPPM good delivery lists, 180
LTCM (Long-Term Capital
    Management), 132
Luxembourg, 39, 44, 45
    Banque centrale du Luxembourg, 45

MACD (moving convergence/
    divergence momentum indicator),
    180
Macro hedge funds, 83
Malaysia, 28t
Malta central bank, 43
Maple leaf, 180
Margin, 119, 181
Margin calls, 181
Mark to market, 181
Market conventions, 90–91
Market makers, 12–13, 67–68, 158
Market making, 66, 90–91
Market orders, 181
Mauritius, 2, 17, 30
Mboweni, Tito, 48
McDonough, William J., 131
MCX (Multi-Commodity Exchange of
    India Ltd.), 181
Metric tonnes, 2, 71
Mexico, 48

Michaud, Richard, 125
Michaud, Robert, 125
Middle East, 116, 120, 121
    (See also individual countries)
Miners of gold [see Producers (miners/
    mining companies)]
Minimum/maximum (min/max),
    181
Mining gold, 149, 150
Monetary authorities, 6, 129
Monetary policy, trust in, 4
Moving average, 181
Moving convergence/divergence
    momentum indicator (MACD),
    180
Multi-Commodity Exchange of India
    Ltd. (MCX), 181
Mutual funds, 83

Naked options, 181
Napoleon, 181
Národná banka Slovenska, 45
National Commodity and Derivatives
    Exchange (NCDX), 182
Netherlands, 17, 27t, 29t, 37, 39, 42
    De Nederlandsche Bank, 42
New York, as trading center, 65, 66
New York Mercantile Exchange
    (NYMEX), 72, 104–107, 182
Newmont, Nevada mine, 150
Nitric acid parting, 184
No Dirty Gold, 160–161
Noble, 182
North America, scrap gold from, 121
North American gold miners, 62
Norway, 17
Numismatics, 182
NYMEX (see New York Mercantile
    Exchange)

Oesterreichisch Nationalbank, 42
Offer, 182
Official sector:
    buyers of gold, 33–36
    countries holding gold, 27–33
    European central bank Gold
        Agreement, 38–51
    perception of gold, 25–27
    selling of gold by central banks,
        36–38
Online gold exchanges, 66, 72, 101–
    104, 107
Open interest, 182

Index

Open outcry, 97–99, 104, 107, 182
Open position, 182
Options, 43, 182
  EcbGA on, 42, 47
  structures of, 82–83
Options market making, 91
Options markets:
  gold, 81–83
  interbank, 85
Ore, 182
Osmium, 182
OTC (over the counter), 182
OTC market (*see* Over-the-Counter market)
OTC (over the counter) options, 183
Out of the money, 62, 183
Over the counter (OTC), 182
Over-the-counter (OTC) options, 183
Over-the-Counter (OTC) market, 67, 71, 72, 104, 107
Overbought, 183
Oversold, 183

Palladium, 183
Palladium fixing, 183
Panda, 183
Panning, 183
Paper gold, 183
Paulson, John, 18
Paulson & Co. hedge fund, 18
"Pay fixed and receive floating," 79
PBoC (People's Bank of China), 30
Pennyweight, 183
Pension funds, 83, 110
People's Bank of China (PBoC), 30
Perception of gold, 25–27
Personal Investment Authority (PIA), 184
Philharmoniker, 183
Philippines, 28t
Physical demand, 14–15, 115–116
Physical gold, 115–122
  consignment stocks, 118–119
  cultural differences in use of, 117–118
  demand for, 14–15, 115–116
  as gift, 120–121
  gold wire and sheets, 123
  investing in, 138–139
  properties of, 193–197
  scrap, 121–122
PIA (Personal Investment Authority), 184

Placer Dome, 41
Platinum, 11–12, 184
Platinum fixing, 184
Platinum group metals, 184
Platinum market, 11
Poehl, Karl Otto, 4
Poland, 16, 29–30
Portable wealth, gold as, 126–128
Portugal, 7, 17, 29t, 39, 42
  Banco de Portugal, 42
Precious metals, 184
Price curve, 59
Price of gold:
  1979 to 2001, 3–4, 3f
  1999, 1, 38
  2000 to mid-2005, 5–6, 5f
  mid-2005 to early 2010, 6–7, 6f, 7f
  conditions for rally in, 7
  conspiracy theories about, 130–135, 159–160
  drivers of (*see* Drivers of gold price)
  and EcbGA, 39–40
  and euro/U.S. dollar exchange rate, 9–11, 10f–11f
  in newspapers, 155
  in OTC markets, 71
  relative to U.S. dollar, 129–130
  relative to U.S. inflation, 4f
  "standard," 155
Producers (miners/mining companies), 40–41, 149
  borrowing of gold by, 54, 56
  China, 12
  by country, 149
  as driver of gold price, 20–21
  and gold option market, 81–82
  and hedging, 5, 40, 41, 54, 56, 58–63, 81–83
  lending of gold to, 54
Properties of gold, 193–197, 194f, 195t, 197t
Pulvermacher, Katharine, 125
Purity of gold:
  cultural differences in, 116
  DGCX trades, 102
  market differences in, 119
  TOCOM trades, 94, 96
Purple gold, 123
Put options, 82, 85, 184
Put spread, 184

Quantos, 82
Quartation, 184

Index

Refining, 184
Relative Strength Index (RSI), 185
Repo, 76–78
Reserve Bank of India, 2, 17
Resistance, 184
Rho, 184–185
Rhodium, 185
Rice-Davies, Mandy, 132
Risk, 72, 185
Rolled gold, 185
Rothschild, N.M., 73–75
RSI (Relative Strength Index), 185
Russia, 3, 16, 17, 27, 27t, 32–34, 34t
    Central Bank of Russia, 26, 32, 125
Ruthenium, 185

Sales of gold:
    by central banks, 1–2, 4–5, 16–17,
        36–38
    and EcbGA, 39, 42, 43, 46, 51–52
    by IMF, 47, 48, 50
    London gold fixing, 74–75
Saudi Arabia, 27
Schweitzerische Nationalbank, 42
Scrap gold, 121–122, 185
Securities and Futures Authority (SFA),
    186
Self Regulatory Organizations (SROs),
    187
Sell signals, 185
Sentiment, 19–20, 121, 137
Settlement date, 43, 185
Settlement price, 185
Settlement risk, 185–186
SFA (Securities and Futures Authority),
    186
SGX (Singapore Exchange Limited),
    186
Shanghai Futures Exchange, 100–101,
    186
Shanghai Gold Exchange, 186
Shark fin, 143
Sheet gold, 123
Short position, 186
Short straddle, 186
Silver, 147–148, 148f, 186
Silver fixing, 186
Silver market, 71
Singapore, 28t
Singapore Exchange Limited (SGX),
    186
Slovakia, 45
    Národná banka Slovenska, 45

Slovenia central bank, 43
Smelting, 186
Société Générale, 73
Souk, 186
South Africa, 11–12, 27, 48–49, 149
South African gold miners, 62
South African Reserve Bank, 48–49
Sovereign (coin), 128, 186
Sovereign debt, 7, 83
Sovereign wealth funds (SWFs), 32,
    35, 83
Spain, 7, 29t, 39, 42
    Banco de España, 42
SPDR Gold Shares, 15, 110, 112–114
Spot deferred, 187
Spot gold trading, 68–71
Spot market making, 90
Spot price, 56
Spot settlement, 187
Sri Lanka, 2, 16, 28t, 30
SROs (Self Regulatory Organizations),
    187
Standard bar/plate/ingot, 187
Standard deviation, 187
"Standard" price of gold, 155
Stochastics, 187
Stop losses, 187
Straddles, 188
Strangles, 188
Strauss-Kahn, Dominique, 49
Strike price, 60, 188
Structured notes, 143–144
Summers, Lawrence H., 131
Suomen Pankki, 42
Supply and demand, 12, 53, 55, 151
Support, 188
Sveriges Riksbank, 42
Swaps, 188
    gold, 76–78
    gold IRSs, 78–79
    lease rate, 58, 78–79
    loco, 156
Sweden, 17, 38, 42
    Sveriges Riksbank, 42
SWFs (see Sovereign wealth funds)
Switch, 188
Switzerland, 1–2, 17, 27t, 29t, 37–38,
    42
    Schweizerische Nationalbank, 42

Tael, 98, 188
Taiwan, 28t
Tamil Nadu, India, 127

Index

Teacher Retirement System of Texas (TRS), 18–19
Technical analysis, 188
Thailand, 28*t*
Theta, 188
Time value, 188
Tokyo Commodities Exchange (TOCOM), 72, 93–97, 107, 189
Tola, 189
Tom/next, 189
Tonnes, 2, 71
TRACKS Gold Shares, 110
  (*See also* SPDR Gold Shares)
Trading centers, major, 65–67, 158
Trading gold:
  against currency, 85
  "rules" for, 147–148
  (*See also* Investing in gold)
Trading gold interest rates, 76–81
Transfer of gold, 86–90, 88*f,* 89*f*
Trend, 189
Trend line, 189
Trichet, Jean-Claude, 49
Troy ounces, 69, 156, 189
TRS (Teacher Retirement System of Texas), 18–19
Turnover, 88–90, 88*f,* 89*f*

UBS AG, 87
Ulyukaev, Alexei, 32
Unallocated gold, 69
Unallocated gold accounts, 70, 140–141, 158, 189
Underlying, 189
United Arab Emirates, 17
United Kingdom, 1–2, 17, 29*t,* 37–38
United States, 4, 22, 27, 27*t,* 29*t,* 149–151
U.S. dollar:
  China's apparent rejection of, 16
  and gold price, 5–7, 7*f,* 9–12, 129–130
  interest on gold in, 56–58

and option market, 85
in post-September 11, 2001, period, 5
safety of, 8

Value date, 189
Vanilla options, 82, 190
Vanilla sales, 62
Vanilla trades, 57
Variation margin, 190
Vega, 190
Venezuela, 27
Vietnam War, 126–127
Virtual Metals Group, 153
Volatility, 190
Volcker, Paul, 4
Volume, 190
Vreneli, 190

Waddell & Reed Financial, Inc., 18
Wafer, 190
WAG (Washington Agreement on Gold), 38
Warehouse receipt, 190
Washington Agreement on Gold (WAG), 38
Weight, 71
Weighted moving average, 190
WGC (*see* World Gold Council)
White gold, 190
Window and anniversary barriers, 82
World Gold Council (WGC), 113, 114, 152
Writer, 191

Xiang Junbo, 26

Yi Gang, 36
Yield curve, 54–56, 191
Yield on gold, 53–54

Zero-cost options, 191
Zurcher Kantonalbank (ZKB), 110, 111*f*

About the Author

Jonathan Spall has worked for Barclays Capital for six years. As the product manager for precious metals, he is responsible for growing the precious metals business and for commodity relationships with central banks and governments on a global basis. He spent ten years at Deutsche Bank, most recently as a London-based director with responsibility for official sector marketing (commodities) and head of metals marketing (Europe/Africa). Spall earlier worked for Deutsche Bank in Hong Kong and Australia as head of metals. A regular speaker at international precious metals conferences, Spall also writes a monthly column for Abu Dhabi's nrewspaper, *The National*, as well as being a columnist for the *Financial Times*.